THE DIVINE LAW

THE DIVINE LAW

GOOD AND EVIL

BY

REVEREND LAWRENCE L. BLANKENSHIP

iUniverse, Inc.
Bloomington

The Divine Law
Good and Evil

iUniverse books may be ordered through booksellers or by contacting:

iUniverse
1663 Liberty Drive
Bloomington, IN 47403
www.iuniverse.com
1-800-Authors (1-800-288-4677)

ISBN: 978-1-4759-5169-1 (sc)
ISBN: 978-1-4759-5170-7 (ebk)

Printed in the United States of America

iUniverse rev. date: 10/18/2012

CONTENTS

PREFACE

This book is written for people interested in Holy Bible. It aims at giving them both an introductory text and a book for future reference, not an exhaustive language. The book is therefore neither strictly a textbook nor a language treatise, but rather a handbook for ready reference.

The authors are convinced that a working knowledge of Hebrew is essential to understanding the Old and New Testaments. Peoples, they have observed, either do not grasp the relevance of language study for their future ministry or else are subjected to an oversimplified language training which does not equip them to make practical use of their knowledge in the study of the Old and New Testaments.

It intent is to bring to the average reader of the Bible, in biblical and nonbiblical terms, the shifted results of the most reliable scholarly study of these healer lyric expressions of good health.

The sixth edition of The Divine Law: Good and Evil is acknowledgment of indebted and sincerely grateful to many individual for their suggestions and criticisms in the preparation of the manuscript, namely, lateRev. E.D. Blankenship Sr., [My Father]; Dr. Herbert J. Vandort; Rev. Johnnie J. Blocker; Mrs. W. L. Blankenship[Mother]; Sis. Zennie M. Blocker; Ms. Katie M. Reese; Mrs. LaRhonda Smith [My Daughter]; Ms. Lucille French [My Daughter], who gave him the benefit of their comments and criticisms after either reading the manuscript or using the preliminary edition as a text in their lives; and certain unknown reviewers for their evaluation and criticism. Finally, the author owes no greater debt of appreciation and gratitude than due God the Father, the Son Jesus Christ, and the Holy Spirit, and his professors, and teacher who taught him.

Also his [Mother], and his [Wife] Zelmer J. Blankenship encouraged through the months of writing and rewriting necessary to get it in its final form.

Reverend Lawrence L. Blankenship

THE AUTHOR

The authors of this book, an former students, who are now had theology training in Hebrew languages, and Greek language, but at the same time he retained a practical outlook. By using a combination of the inductive and deductive method, he begin the reading of Genesis very early in the course in this book, and during the year students acquire definit language principles, a basic vocabulary, and the ability to read Bible Hebrew, and Greek. The authors are to be commended for having made available in book form the results of their experience and for giving a wider public the benefit of his achievements.

The teaching of the Word of God in the original Bible should be of perennial interest, especially for the minister who wishes to unfold the riches of the Bible. In too many instances, however, Bible should been taught as though it actually were a "Good" book, and this attitude has been reflected in the methods of instruction student. Consequently, the results of teaching the Bible in theological seminaries have frequently been very been very disappointing. Sometimes so many words details were presented that the student never had an opportunity of covering any ground in reading the word of God.

In other cases, for the sake of minimizing the study of the student, Bible is not taught systematically, and in consequence the difficulty of the language would increased and in the end the student became courage or strength. It is said that the theological student would use Bible language only for exegetical purposes or for making word studies in order to find theological conceptions.

By this method, however, the student never got a grasp of the word, and from the very beginning he or she was defeated in his or her purpose of using Bible for exegesis. Those teachers overlooked the fact thatr word studies and expositions based on the original demand the ability to enter into the spirit of the word of the Bible. The great ideas of the Old Testament are enshrined in words, and the key to them is found in a working knowledge of the Bible.

INTRODUCTION

The aim of the present book Good and Evil. What Rev. Blankenship has done so admirably for the Law of God and The Law of The State Vol. 1 and 2, a previous volume of this series. Some change in the method of treatment has been inevitable in view of the radical differences between the two parts of our Bible. The Good and evil is concerned with God, Satan, Sinful Diseases, and Seven Deadly Sins cannot be rightly understood without some knowledge of general history during the millennium before Jesus Christ. The Bible is not only a book for Christians but a national literature, which needs to be studied, like any other literature, from an esthetic and historical point of view. In the Bible the belief purpose is everything. What we seek from it, almost to the exclusions of all else, is a first hand knowledge of the origin and nature of the Christian belief.

In the following Chapter 1, I am explain God's word to a novice in the field and to help such a person obtain an understanding of the Good and Evil. It is hoped that Christian institute utilizing this book as a text will augment it with codes of method. The book is intended as a scholarly treaded, or an exhaustive study. It is intended to be a readable and instructive guide through a field which is too often made mysterious, Good and Evil. This book is intended for the believe and unbelievable to area of God's goodness and resolution of disputes by their use. Persistence reviewing the subject and practice of evil should lead the reader into thinking, the most important part of being a believe in Jesus Christ. It is also my hope that after serving as a learning device in church, this book will also be helpful to the practicing study as a reference source. The are of good is, however, a complex and exhaustive discipline. This book should never be used as a final authoritative source for learning. In reading you will learn about God, Satan, Sinful

Diseases, and Seven Deadly Sins, which are only touched upon in this book.

What makes God's so interesting is that God's does not changing and that there are rarely answer which are absolutely right. It takes many years of study and practice to become a competent theology; you cannot expect to become one by reading this one book, complete and consummate as it is. However, the vast fund of information will make you a judicious layman on all spiritual problems. In addition to the practical spiritual knowledge you will also obtain a perfect understanding of your limitations and will not, therefore, dispense with the church services when really needed. You shall also learn from the pastor limitations which are an inevitable result of the present day unintegrated medical research and of the consequent baffling state and deficiency of medical knowledge. By acquiring these understandings, you will never fall victims to untrained preacher who preach falsely.

CHAPTER 1

God

The study of the place of God in the history of human culture must begin with the Old Testament. This is not simply for the self-evident reason that all representation of Him since of the creative process, have claimed to be based on the Old Testament; although there are many evident about God. But we shall not understand the history of God, unless we begin by considering the nature and literary form of the sources that have come down to us in volume of a book. God is the usual name for the supreme power in the universe, the source of all other existences, the controller of the creative process, the moving influence in the pattern followed by history, and the object of man's highest reverence and aspiration. We believe that the reality of such a God is a demand of the pure reason. most of the great believe, especially the Jewish and Christian, teach that God is known only as He reveals Himself, and that the organ of this revelation is Faith.

If the Scriptures be regarded as a record of this revelation, then we must regard it as progressive, there is a profound difference between God and Satan. Theology proper, the first half of this article has been a brief summary of what the Bible says about God. Its statements are deceptively simple in form, the ideas are profound and their implications have puzzled many minds, both devout and irreligious. Therefore the descriptive method of biblical theology must give way to a more systematic and philosophic analysis. But again, as the descriptive summary was brief, so too this second half can barely indicate the labor of centuries on these problems. Only three types of problem will be mentioned: Theology, Science, and Ethics. Since the Bible everywhere asserts the existence of God, the first question of systematic or philosophic theology concerns the proof of this assertion. Does our belief in God's existence depend solely on Scriptural authority or does it depend on some sort of proof? If the latter, is the proof, a direct mystical experience of God, or is it a syllogistic process that starts with observation of nature? The present writer believes that the argument is worthless because (1) it is circular, in that the existence of God is itself used to disprove an infinite series of causes, with disproof is necessary to prove the existence of God; (2) its premises use the term existence in a spatial and temporal sense, while the conclusion uses the term in a different sense; and (3) as argument from effect to cause can assign to the cause only sufficient attributes to account for the effect by which alone it is known, and this would give us a God who is neither omnipotent, omniscient, nor perfectly righteous. It is not based on an observation of nature but on an analysis of the concept of God. As a man or woman who would deny that a triangle contains 180 degrees simply does not understand the meaning of triangle, so one who denies the existence of God has not grasped the concept of God. God as the being than whom a greater cannot be conceived, cannot be conceived not to exist; for if God could be conceived not to exist, it would be possible to conceive of an existing being greater that God; but to conceive of a being greater that the being than whom a greater cannot be conceived is a self-contradiction.

The important question therefore is not, Is there a God? Of course there is. But the important question is. What is God? Now, we are looking at the description of biblical theology. Although the proofs of God's existence have been prominent the theological discussion, they are but part of a more general problem. Can God be known? Some secular philosophers have asserted the existence of unknowable entities. A philosophic absolute may be thought to be transcendent as to be beyond thought. Or, as the human mind, taking its rise from sensory experience may be essentially incapacitated to know much if anything of an eternal being. Or, more popularly, the finite mind cannot grasp the infinite. Those who assert the existence of unknowable object seem to contradict themselves, for if the object were quite unknowable, one could not know either that it existed or that it was unknowable. Than too this type of philosophy is usually suspected of making all knowledge impossible, even knowledge of the weather. Some philosophers have taught that all knowledge consists of sensory images. If so, man or woman never have a concept of God because God is not a sense object and no image of Him is possible. Either than a believe in God must reject empiricism and find some a prior basis of knowledge, as he or she must struggle, as Thomas did, with such little success, to bridge the chasm between concepts abstracted from sensation and a knowledge of the timeless and space less spirit. The impossibility of knowing what God is has also been argued from a theory of definition.

When an apple tree or a squirrel is defined, it is placed in a genus. An apple tree is a species of rose, and a squirrel is a species of rodent. But God is not a species of any genus. "To whom then will ye liken God? Or what likeness will ye compare unto him?" The point that I making is that God is incomparable, and therefore all making of images of Him is absurd. I am speaking both to my fellow clergyman, Christians, and non-Christian, who has not being seduced to idolatry by imposing statutes of deities all about them, and to the heathen themselves. He is satirical both here and in subsequent descriptions of idol manufacturing. It is not difficult to show how ludicrous are likenesses in metal, wood, or stone, of the God of the universe. But Isaiah 40:18 question is not fully answered by exposing the folly of idolatry. A basic conviction of Christian faith is involved here. It is through images that intercourse between persons becomes possible.

We may say that we "see" one another. In fact, we see tiny images which rays of light refract upon the retina of the eye. Through these diminutive images we do business and form friendship. In men or women's intercourse with God they are impelled to form images of Him. There is nothing wrong in such image making; but an unworthy or inadequate mental image is tragic, because it thwarts God's desired fellowship with his children. Revelation is his effort to convey a correct impresssion of himself. The folly is in resting in man made conceptions of God, instead of responding to his own disclosure of himself. It is not for us to devise a likeness, but to accept his self-portrait. Isaiah question found its answer centuries later when, out of the church's experience of Christ, an apostle called him "the image of the invisible God" in Col. 1:15, and another heard him saying, "He that hath seen me hath seen the Father" in John 14:9. Since knowledge of what a thing is, its definition, it follows that God cannot be know.

The theist, to avoid this conclusion, must produce a different theory of definition, and its desirability may be emphasized by pointing out that if species only can be defined and known, genera, especially the highest genera or genus, remain unknown. Moses said, "The secret things belong unto the Lord our God; but those thing which are revealed belong unto us and our children forever". The Bible, therefore, both here and everywhere, assumes that we can know some truths without knowing all truths. Accordingly it is incumbent upon us to develop an epistemology in which the relationship are not such as to limit us to the disjunction of total ignorance or omniscience. This epistemology may follow Christian view that Christ is the light of every man or woman; that is, mankind possesses as an a priori endowment at least the rudiments of knowledge, so that whenever anyone knows anything he or she is in contact with God, who is truth.

These are some of the names of God. (1) El is the divine being, the highest God, possessor or Creator of Heaven and Earth, as in Gen. 33:20, was known by Jacob and not Esau who, notwithstanding many contrary indications, was to become the decisive figure in the history of Israel. He was called it El-Elohe-Israel. It was dedicated to God, as God's chastening yet redeeming power has been revealed to him at Peniel. Not by any virtue of what he was, but by the purpose of God which would work through him, his life would be significant. On the other hand, some Christians have explained the plural as an anticipation of the Trinity. But again, without a commonly used singular no one in Old Testament times could have developed Trinitarian ideas from the word alone. The plural would suggest polytheism more readily than trinitarianism were it not for hints other than the word itself being used with a singular verb. This is not to say that material in the Old Testament cannot hint at some distinctions within the Godhead. Though the etymology is obscure, the word may have come from a root meaning strong. In any case, this name is used chiefly in connection with God's governance of the world and mankind in general.

Remember El, which is not related directly to Elohim, occurs more than 200 times, chiefly in Job, Psalms, and Isaiah. It is often accompanied by some descriptive term or in such combinations as El-Shaddai, God Almighty, or El-Elyon, God Most High. (2) Yhwh (Yahweh) in contrast with this most general name of Hebrew word God, unlike Jehovah. (3) Jehovah is an artificial English word put together from the four Hebrew consonants and the vowels of the Hebrew word Adonai, or Lord. Before the time of Christ the Jews developed a superstitious dread of pronouncing JHVH; when they came to it in the Bible, they pronounced Adonai instead; then later the vowels of Adonai were written into the manuscripts, and in modern times people have been saying Jehovah. Jehovah is the name used in connection with God's choice of, revelation to, and special care for his covenant people. It is term almost always used in Theophanous, and almost always revelation is the word of JHVH. Jehovah is the redemptive name of God. As you may know, higher criticism has often tried to maintain that one author could not possibly have used both names for God, and that therefore the first chapter of Genesis was written by one man and the second by another.

The theory of two authors is not needed to explain the use of these two names. The first chapter tells of God's general relation to the world, and then the second begins to relate his special are for men who by Adam's fall soon were in need of redemption. God in his wisdom furnished these two names as a convenient method of summarizing what the Scriptures teach about God; Elohim, his work of creation; and Jehovah, his work of redemption. (4) "I am that I am". That is to say, God is one who exists and who can never cease to exist. The word of Exodus 3:14 however, represents only one tradition, the so-called priestly. A different tradition, the so-called Jahwist, makes the name a great deal earlier than Moses. What Moses learned at the burning bush was the complete dependability of this word; the certainty that he will carry out His agreements. The word is one who can be relied upon; He is utterly trustworthy. He is not fickle, like the gods of other nations. He is the same yesterday, today, and forever. This was the God who had called Abraham. He was the God whom the early Hebrews thought of as their own national God and special guardian, without disputing the right of other peoples to have Gods of their own. We need to know more about the word God spoken to Moses concerning the children of Israel, "I Am That I Am" was God own words unto Moses; and it was a short one, to confound mortality, that durst question God, or ask him what He was. It should be notice, if the name of the God I worship is I Am, it seems to follow that only through what I am can I worship Him right. God and the archangel Michael were in one of the anterooms of heaven. In a continuous torrents all the prayers, oral and sung, of mankind were ascending from earth. It was a baby of sound in all tongues, and on all sides of every question, hurricanes of passionate demands, winds of speech whining with wheedling words, gusts of insistent requests for special favors. Overwhelmed with it all, Michael said to God, "If you will allow me, Sire, I would say that you made a great take when you let man learn to talk. If he was not able to talk, it would be possible then for you to know what he was really praying for". And God said, "I do not listen to their words. I listen only to their lives". God closed the window and opened the door, and all the tempest of words stopped. Instead from the earth came up clearly another prayer.

Most of it was distressing, but a weak, wavering voice did arise also from the lives of men and women to heaven. Notice the prayer them pray, "O Lord, if it does not cost us too much, we sometimes would like to be just and courageous and kind. Amen". For the only prayer of mine that rises above the roof is the prayer of what I Am. In this affirmation also is the pledge and proof of our existential unity with God and with one another, as the author puts it. It is strange that, though we all say our "I am", we nevertheless fancy ourselves to be so far, so essentially, separated from on another. Is not the same spirit in all of us which from our thousand mouths says his "I am", thus proving himself and us true? (5) God as Creator, the Bible of Genesis gives the impression that, aside from God himself, everything that exists has been created. God alone is self-existent. nothing else exists of own right, independently, or without beginning. This initial impression is corroborated by many later passages read Neb. 9:6.

(6) Trinity is the union of three divine Persons in the Godhead. The term means that the divine life is characterized by interior personal relationships; whose sources are described as Father, Son, and Holy Spirit. It is true that Christianity speaks of the Father as the First Person, and of the Son as the Second Person, and of the Holy Spirit as the Third Person; but (first, second, and third, here do not represent a time order, rather the order of necessary relationships. It is of the nature of the Son to depend on the Father and it is the nature of the Holy Spirit to depend on the Father and Son. (7) Redemption, the act of redeeming, or the state of being redeemed. The root meaning of the word (redeem), is "TO SET FREE", or "TO CAUSE TO BE SET FREE". Sometimes an offering or a gift is required as a condition to the release. The Bible there deals with redemption in two different ways: sometimes it means what men or women do for themselves or

for each other to effects deliverance from danger, and in particular to regain the lost favor of God; and sometimes it means a deliverance that comes to men and women because of the gracious activity of God on their behalf.

The grace of God is not absent from the transactional concept; but it is understood as grace that inclines God to accept one thing in place of another, especially an offering instead of an inflicted loss or punishment. In the concept, however, which sees God as Himself the Redeemer who effect the redemption or brings about the release, the grace is much more apparent, because God provides on his own account the means necessary to set men and women free especially freedom from sin, from sinning, and from the fruits of sin.

The Christian redemption is a redemption for which Jesus Christ paid the price. The eternal Father gives from within Himself His eternal Son to redeem men and women from bondage, primarily spiritual men or women from bondage, set free, from a power greater than themselves, and it is this that God sets Himself to accomplish in Jesus Christ. It cannot be accomplished without cost; but God lays the cost upon Himself, since what the Son endures the Father also endures, and both endure it from the same motive of holy love.

God had a multitude of name as many as men and women could invent. According to the Christian view, the gulf between man and woman and God is bridged by Jesus Christ, who partakes of the nature of both. He is both Son of God and Son of Man. This implies that God is self-revealed in Jesus Christ, consequently that the qualities of God's character and the nature of his purpose are fully seen in him. The crucifixion of Jesus Christ as a sacrifice of the Lamb of God to satisfy the justice of the Father brings out one further feature of deity. At the beginning the personality of God was pointed out.

Now it is evident that God is not one Person, but more than one. If the son is sent from heaven, while the Father is not sent; if the Father loves the Son and the Son loves the Father,; if the Son sacrifices himself or prays a ransom to the Father; it follows that the Father and the Son are different Persons. Every true pastor, prophet from Moses to Malachi preached with all the vehemence and power he possessed to turn the people from the evil world.

In order to understand God from different Religion, it is well to begin as far back in time as we can go. We turn therefore briefly to others gods. could we find answers to these questions, they might help us to determine when and how other gods began. But is not certain. Because other gods is a product of the earliest attempt of the human mind to achieve a sense of security in the world, the names of as follows: Islamite, Hinduism, and Buddhism or Jain; man may have been the first to create their gods. The god of the Greek religion is Zeus. But others gods are under the Lord God Almighty, who created the heavens and the earth, has a power and control that is universal in extent and total in depth. Omnipotence, first seen in creation, is stated and exemplified throughout the Bible.

All the miracles come to mind. When Abraham despaired of having a son by his wife Sarah, God introduced his promise by saying, "I am the Almighty God" and "Is anything too hard for the Lord" Gen. 17:1; 18:14. The kind of conscience which is created in men and women aware of God can give the understanding justice which is necessary for the solution of industrial disputes. And only this conscience in statesmen and the public opinion of common men and women can ultimately create world cooperation and world peace.

Education integrated around the sought meaning of God can give wisdom instead of disjointed bits of information, and produce a personality profoundly integrated and profoundly energized. For the individual at any moment the problems of life may seem overwhelming, but the Bible can widen our perspective. God has made a covenant with many souls, and those souls have not been disappointed. There is a communion of the saints, living and dead. When any man or woman tries to be worthy of that his or her life is lifted up into a spiritual companionship which gives it dignity. If we believe is Almighty God here is the ultimate guarantee of a life that shall be significant.

The profoundly Christian understanding knew well the limitations and frailties of man and woman, but it had been gripped by the amazing faith that man or woman in his or her weakness can yet have behind him or her infinite strength of God. A man or woman is not to be made more confident himself or herself; he or she can be confident because he or she has a covenant with another. By mechanical processes men and women carry on the habitual attitudes of inherited character, but the Old Testament seers knew that character was first created, and can be long sustained, only through a life-giving consciousness of God.

That God is, that he enters into relationship with human souls, that all worth while inspiration comes from him this was the Christian faith.

The glory of that inheritance should not be lost. Remember Christian is not a human notion, a pathetic projection of human wishes which may or may not find a divine response. On the contrary, it is God moving toward man or woman and giving to the bond between them therefore the eternal assurance of his own purpose. God spoke first to Abraham, not Abraham first to God. God spoke first to Moses, not Moses to God; God spoke first to Isaiah, not Isaiah to God, God spoke first to Jeremiah, not Jeremiah to God, to all the inspired souls. Great Christian experience always rests in the certainty that the soul has not gone out into an empty universe where all that it would hear would be the echo of its own cry, but that the Lord of the universe has come into the soul itself and spoken there. That is the eternal truth which was trying to voice itself in the doctrine of predestination; the truth of the priority of God. The aspirations of human hearts are not just the pathetic smoke of a self kindled fire; they are the answering flame that has been lighted by the fire that has come down from on high. Consider the difference this makes for moral and spiritual courage. To all Christians, you need to say, I want God and I am willing to try to draw near to him if only He will let me" is one thing; and there is only feeble influence in it. To hear it promised that God himself draws near is something else, and in it there is assurance that nothing can upset.

CHAPTER 2

Satan

The Bible gives us the history of Evil from Heaven and Earth. The history of mankind was divided into two periods: (1) The present age and the future age, which New Testament called, the world and the world to come. This world is subject to Satan, devil, the god of evil of this world, the prince of this world, and evil spirits. (2) The world to come will begin after the end of this evil world, this world will be happy. Historically this unique relationship between Jesus Christ and Satan began in Heaven. Satan was an angel of the Lord God, and he love God. According to the first Chapter of Genesis 1:26, "And God said, Let us make man in our image, after our likeness; and let them have dominion over the fish of the sea, and over the fowl of the air, and over the cattle, and over all the earth, and over every creeping thing the creepeth upon the earth". At this point Satan, and Jesus begin to exchange words about the word "us" and "our image". Satan says, God said, let us make man in our image, Jesus answer Satan saying, God did not mean you; He means the Trinity the Godhead. Satan disagreed with Jesus about the Trinity. God used the words "us" and "our image". So Satan believes that mean him. Satan and Jesus began a heated argument about the words "us" and "our image". The argument over the words "us" and "our image" called problem between Jesus and Satan. Satan dislike Jesus Christ very much, but he love God. This is why God said in verse 27, "So God created man in His own image, in the image of God created he him; male and female created he them" God stop the argument between Satan and Jesus Christ. Because of the arguments between Satan and Jesus Christ war begin in heaven. Satan created "Sin" and "Hate" in heaven and fight between the angels of God's and

Satan angels. So God said to Michael in Revelation 12:7-9-12 reads, "And there was war in Heaven: Michael and his angels fought against the dragon; and the dragon fought and his angels. And the great dragon was cast out, that Old Serpent, called Devil, and Satan, which deceiveth the whole world: he was out into the earth, and his angels were cast out with him. Therefore rejoice, ye heavens, and ye that dwell in them. Woe the inhabiters of the earth and of the sea! For the devil is come down unto you, having great wrath, because he knoweth that he hath but a shot timer. Satan the ruler of super-human beings or personified powers usually conceived as malevolent. The awareness of the ominous element in human experience is expressed in terms of hostile numinous beings who threaten human well-being, either in this life or beyond. In this context, the human situation is thought to reflect a transcendent conflict between opposing powers of good and evil.

It should be know that God called Satan that Old Serpent. Satan was transform as Serpent. The description of the serpent is a serious reckoning with the fact of sin. Evil enters into the world, and once here it is dangerous and may be deadly. Moreover, as the author wrote Genesis story he knew, it may be more deadly than it seems. Observe that in this account the serpent is not at first repulsive. He comes with plausible argument. He comes with a kind of insinuating grace.

At the beginning of the story the man. God said let "us" make man in our image, after our likeness". Satan was not involve in the created proceed. The Old Testament contains only three explicit references to Satan as a distinct personality I Chronicles 21:1; Zechariah 3:1-2. Job 1:7 tell us about Jesus Christ and Satan at the house of Job, and Satan's idea verse 9. This is not a rational view. It is a Spiritual view. Jesus Christ on His part undertakes, as one might look with a patient smile on a jaundiced lad, to point out that surely matters on earth are not so bad as Satan would have everybody think, and gently reminds him of Job as a case in point. Recall Gen. 1:1, and notice the addition to it here. The disasters which follow are nevertheless attributed by Job as well as by the friends to God himself. There was no ultimate dualism in the Hebrew mind. There was no knowledge of "secondary causes", which for us seem to postpone the perplexity at least until we can turn the page; no nice distinctions between "absolute will" and "contingent will". Verse 7 "And the Lord said unto Satan, Whence comest thou? Then Satan answered the Lord, and said, From going to and fro in the earth, and from walking up and down in it"; with his hands in his pockets, his tongue in his check, and a shrug of his shoulders,: From all over". Satan seems to have had no particular province allotted to him, as some of the others had. His is a roving commission. Satan is a kind of ambassador at large. There is not yet about him any of the full-blown malevolence of the figure that writes and flashes its way through the drawings of Blake. This is not Milton's fallen angel, Lucifer, son of the morning; nothing nearly so magnificent as that captain of heaven's rebellious legions, standing there in Paradise lost, stripped of all his honors. Please notice Satan of Job is a kind of devil in the making, already more enamored of his faultfinding than is quite decent. Satan can fairly be seen kicking up the stare dust and looking around with a smirk, as if the cynicism he harbors in his heart were a sweet morsel on his tongue. Satan does not think too highly of Jesus Christ government; much less has man or been able to pull the wool over his eyes.

Satan is the "nobody's child" of the universe, who has seen it all and likes none of it. It is the mention of Job that sets him off. Some said, why does God permit evil? On verse 6 give us the answer. We find that Job was not a problem for the mind to tease; it was a problem for the soul to wrestle with. The wisdom of this book, and indeed of the Holy Bible, and of Jewish literature, has to do with life and not with logic. It has to do with the sweeping passions of the human heart, with the stalwart qualities of the human will, and not alone with the calculating processes of the human mind, which incidentally may well belong more to the mind itself than to whatever it is in the universe that is ultimately real.

Good and evil present at the time of Job, as it is today. Remember Satan is a high archangelic creature who, before the creation of the human race, rebelled against the Creator and became the chief antagonist of God and man. In Daniel 10:13, and Ephesians 6:12. In their full scope these passages paint Satan's past career as Lucifer, and as the Anointed Cherub, in his pre-fall splendor. They portray as well his apostasy in drawing with him a great multitude of lesser celestial creatures. In Revelation 12:4 reads, "And his tail drew the third part of the stars of heaven, and did cast them to the earth: and the dragon stood before the woman which was ready to be delivered, for to devour her child as soon as it was born.

These fallen angels "Demons" fit into two classes: (1) Those that are free and; (2) Those that are bound. The former roam the heaven lies with their prince leader Satan in Matthew 12:24. The angels "Demons" that are bound are evidently guilty of more heinous wickedness and are incarcerated in Tartarus. II Peter 2:4 reads, "For if God spared not the angels that sinned, but cast them down to hell, and delivered them into chains of darkness, to be reserved unto judgment. In Jude 1:6 reads, "And the angels which kept not their first estate, but left their own habitation, he hath reserved in everlasting chains under darkness unto the judgment of the great day." We find, many theologians connect these imprisoned demons with fallen angels who (cohabited) with mortal women in Genesis 6:1-5. The Bible doctrine of Satan is not a copying of Persian dualism as some school unsoundly allege. Although Satan, even after his judgment in the cross, continues to reign as a usurper, and works in tempting and accusing men and women in Rev. 12:10, he is to be ousted from the heavenlies in Rev. 12:7-12, as well as the earth in Rev. 5:1; 19:16, and is to be confined to the abyss for a thousand years in Rev. 20:1-3. When Satan released from the abyss at the end of the thousand years, Satan will make one last made attempt to lead his armies against God in Rev. 20:8-9.

This will eventuate in his final doom when Satan is cast into the lake of fire in Rev. 20:10, which has been prepared for him and his wicked angelic accomplices in Matt. 25:41. This will be the one place where evil angels and unsaved men, women, and children will be kept and quarantined so that the rest of God's sinless universe will not be corrupted in the eternal state. I wrote before "Why does God permit Evil? Satan's present work is widespread and destructive. God permits Satan evil activity for the time being.

Demons must do Satan's bidding. The unsaved are largely under Satan's authority, and Satan rules them through the evil world system over which Satan is head and of which the unregenerate are a part. As far as the saved are concerned, Satan clashes in conflict with them, tempts them and seeks to corrupt and destroy their testimony and even their physical life. Satanic and demonic fury unleashed against the incarnate Jesus Christ. The power of a sinless humanity called forth special satanic temptation of our Lord Jesus Christ. The full glow of light manifested in the earthly life of him who was "the light of the world" exposed the darkness of the powers of evil.

This is the explanation of the unprecedented outburst of demonism that is described in the Gospel narratives. It was because God anointed

Jesus of Nazareth "with the Holy Spirit and with power" that he went about doing good and healing all that were oppressed by the devil. The Bible also teach as a whole therefore, seems to mean that there is a malign power of evil at work in the work, attempting to pervert the purposes of God, especially His purpose for mankind; but there is a limit to the evil power. Against it God employs all his resources, and his chief resource is Jesus Christ, who was "manifested, that he might destroy the works of the devil. Also, whosoever is born of God doth not commit sin; for his or her seed remained in him or her: and he or she cannot sin, because they is born in God. In this the people of God are manifest, and the people of the evil. Whosoever doth not righteousness is not of God, neither he that loveth not his brother. Remember Satan is high archangelic creature who, before the creation of the human race, rebelled against the Creator and became the chief antagonist of God and man.

Satan caused the fall of the human race. His judgment was predicted in Eden read Genesis 3:14, when the nature of evil is disclosed. After evil has had its way its real nature begins to be revealed. It is not clear what the serpent is supposed to have looked like at first, but evidently its looks were pleasant. Then it turned into something different. Upon thy belly shalt thou go, and dust shalt thou eat all the days of thy life. The serpent now is obviously the snake. In our world of physical experience there is nothing from which men or women have a more natural revulsion than from the snake. It is secret and stealthy. It strikes without warning and its bite has poison in it. Only a fool will walk carelessly where snakes lurk. many men, women, and children have come to their senses when God has intervened to show the nature of sin, for then its reality is unmistakably abhorrent mean "hateful".

The evil that somehow is in our world cannot be whistled off. It shall bruise man or woman, and children heel. A man or woman cannot think he or she will escape the fact of sin by acting as if it were not there. It will strike at him or her and wound him or her. When it does wound him or her the effect must be dealt with drastically, as with the bite of a snake. There may be need of quick, sharp moral surgery to keep the poison of sin from spreading. Much contemporary religious thinking has emphasized anew the fact of sin and man's vulnerability to it. The serpent may bruise man or woman's heel, but ultimately man or woman is meant to crush the serpent's head. The Old and

New Testaments has in it always a virile optimism. It is not blind to the tragedy of life, but all the while it looks forward to triumph. Men, women, and nations in their struggles against temptation and in their warfare against evil are meant not to surrender but to prevail. Man and woman is subject to the poisonous fangs of sin but he or she can crush sin if he or she is so determined. These are some of the names of the Satan: (1) Satan is high archangel creature who, before the creation of the human race, rebelled against the Creator and became the chief antagonist of God and man.

Satan caused the fall of the human race in Gen. 3. His judgment was predicted in Eden in Gen. 3:15, and this was accomplished at the cross in John 12:31-33. Satan created his power was third only to Jesus Christ. other names are: Lucifer". (2) Lucifer is a name given the planet Venus when it is the morning star. It is used in Isaiah 14:12 reads, "How art thou fallen from heaven, O Lucifer, son of the morning! How are thou cut down to the ground, which didst weaken the nations. The Hebrew "the shining one" applied to the king of Babylon, fallen from his high estate.

The saying of Jesus "I beheld Satan as lightning fall from heaven". Hence Lucifer came to be regarded as the name of Satan before his fall. Other names are "Devil". (3) Devil is the personification of wickedness incarnate evil; else where the word translated devil, it mean "demon was originally, as in Homer, a god or deity, and the word is used once in this sense in the New Testament. The New Testament demons afflict men and women with mental, moral, and physical distempers. They enter into men or women control them in demon possession, instigate (doctrines of demons) exercise power in the government of the satanic world system; energize idolatry, immorality and human wickedness. Inspire false teachers. I John 4:1-2 reads, "Beloved, believe not every spirit, but try the spirits whether they are of God: because many false prophets are gone out into the world. Hereby know ye the Spirit of God. Every spirit that confesseth that Jesus Christ is come in the flesh is of God. Other names are "Evil one". (5) Evil one is the antithesis of good, and the possibility of its eradication from the soul of man, were prominent in the thought of the minds which produced the Bible. The origin of evil remains one of the greatest moral problems, which challenges man and woman to heroic quests for the truth concerning it. The following tenets bearing upon evil have been accepted by many

Christian thinkers. Physical evil is radically different from moral evil, though much of it is due to moral evil and might be avoided. Many physical evils have value, however, in training character. Evil began when spirits, created free, chose to do evil rather rights, and thus condemned themselves.

This does not discourage God, who has ready a plan of redemption through a self-sacrificing savious. Evil one knows that the revelation of this saviourhood could not have taken place without a conflict between good and evil. Evil is thus made a partner of good, which will ultimately triumph through the infinite patience of God, who allows His creatures to mature into holiness. Man and woman learns to trust God so completely in Christ Jesus that he or she is confident that even a universe with evil in it will finally crown God's total creative acts with a complete vindication of His purpose.

Other names are "Dragon". (6) Dragon a mythical monster depicted in the literature of the ancient Middle East. It is akin to the subtle serpent, and is openly called the great dragon, that Old Serpent, the Devil, and Satan, which deceiveth the whole world. The New Testament antichrist is the same subtle beast that destroyed man's first Eden. The dragon was pictured sometimes as a river-dwelling monster like the alligator or crocodile inhabiting the Nile and denoting Pharaoh himself. The iconography of the Far East, however, depicts the dragon as a symbol of strength and virtue, denoting the coming of spring and rain a once worshipped river beast.

Other names are "Beast". (7) Beast is used symbolically in Daniel and Revelation for empires and powers hostile to God and His people. The "Four Beasts" of Rev. 4:6-9 are more correctly rendered living creatures it also known as Antichrist. Other names are "Antichrist". (8) Antichrist an antagonist of Christ Jesus, who denies that Jesus Christ is the Christ, but who will be conquered for all time by the Second Coming of Christ. Although mentioned by name only in I John: 2:18-22, and 4:3, or II John 7, it is thought to be referred to as "man" II Thessalonians 2:1-12 and as "beast" in Rev. 13 and 17. The concept of a conflict between the forces of good and evil appeared in a very early Babylonian myth, became a dominant part of Persian though, and made its way into Jewish beliefs and Christian doctrine concerning the Second Advent. Early Christians associated antichrist with false teachers and disciples and with apostasies and impious denials of God.

In the ideal or symbolic view, antichrist is an ageless personification of evil, not identifiable with one nation, institution, or individual. It's also known as Abomination or Desolation. Other names are "Serpent". (9) Serpent is a snake of which there are 30 or more species in Palestine and the desert areas South of this region. In the Bible serpent are called by almost a dozen names in addition to the generic (nachash). The serpent of the garden of Eden in Genesis 3:1-4-13, is a symbol of evil. John the Baptist mentioned the viper in his condemnation of the Pharisees and scribes in Matt. 3:7. Many snakes of the Near East are harmless; others have a fiery bite in Isaiah 14:29 and Proverbs 23:32.

In Greek mythology it had long been associated with Aesculapius, deity of healing, and is today a symbol of the medical profession. Other names are "Abomination". Abomination is offensive to God and His plan for man and woman's righteous way of life. Whether (clean) items of tabooed food in Lev. 11 and worship of idols in I Kings 11:15 and harlotry in Rev. 17:5 or dishonesty in Micah. 6:10. Various Old Testament peoples had their own types of conduct (abominable), to the Hebrew ideal.

A fool is described in Prov. 26:25 as having seven abominations in his heart. Other names are Abomination of Desolation". Abomination of Desolation, both words referred to several times in Daniel 8:13; 9:27; 11:31 and 12:11 as an apocalyptic figure, idol, or expression of an idea set up in the sanctuary with baleful effect.

This is now generally thought to refer to the proscription of the Jewish believe by Antiochus Epiphanes and to his setting up in the Temple of an altar to the Olympian Zeus, just prior to the Maccabean revolt. Just what Jesus had in mind when he spoke of an abomination of desolation. Mark 13:14, which would be a sign of the beginning of the Messianic Age is uncertain. It may have been a statute of a Roman emperor, an inappropriate figure, or an event. In United States of America and other county today, we come to a point in our history where hate is maintain.

Other names are "Ku-Klux Klan". Ku-Klux Klan is a Secret Society of white men found in the Southern States after the (Civil War), to re-establish and maintain white supremacy. It should be notice that before the Ku-Klux-Klan, it was a Secret Society group founded by a

King in the seventeenth and eighteenth century. This Secret Society protection the boundaries and has a king that is shared by all the people, and nation.

History says, the king die, and his son became king. The Secret Society stop protection the boundaries of others nation. The nation paid for protection from the Secret Society group. The king son turn out to be hatred toward other people and nation. History says, the Secret Society group ending the long region to terror, and the territory was destroyed. The most ominous expression of protest against the new urban culture was the rebirth of the Ku-Klux Klan. On Thanksgiving nigh in 1915, on Stone Mountain in Georgia, Colonel William L. Simmons and thirty-four followers founded the modern Klan. Only "native born", white gentile Americans, were permitted to join "The Invisible Empire, Knights of the Ku-Klux Klan. Membership grew slowly during World War I, but after 1920, fueled by postwar fears and shrewd promotional techniques, the Klan mushroomed. The Klan demonstrating their hatred against blacks, aliens, Jews, and Catholics, and other races spoke different languages, worshipped in strange churches and lived in distant, threatening cities.

The Klan struck back by coming together and enforcing their values. they punished blacks and other races who did not know their place, women who practiced the new morality, and aliens who refused to conform. beating, flogging, burning with acid even murder were condoned. They also tried more peaceful methods of coercion, formulating codes of behavior and seeking community wide support. Other names are "Skin-Head". Skin-Head is a person who is bald or has his hair shared off or closely cropped. This is a group of working class British youth of late 1960's and the 1970's with closely cropped hair, often engaging in rowdyism.

Rowdy is a person whose behavior is rough, quarrelsome and disorderly; having the nature of or characteristic of a rowdy. They need to be supremacy, the quality or state of being supreme, a supreme power or authority. Sometime they use the act of terrorizing, use of force or threats to demoralize, intimidate, and such use as a political weapon of policy. the demoralization and intimidation produced in power of authority. All races have a Secret Society group who protect their peoples. Birth of a Nation's depiction of the Klan as saving white civilization from bestial blacks and others race inspired vigorous protects from the recently founded National Association for the Advancement of Colored People (NAACP), and censors in few northern cities deleted some of the more blatantly racist scenes. Black race demonstrating their hatred against White, to protect their inherit. Mexican race demonstrating their hatred against While and Black to protect their inherit. Japanese, and China races demonstration their hatred against white, black, and Mexican race to protect their inherit.

People today are reader about "Reconstruction Era". Satan is used different races to destroy each others. Changing views of reconstruction will not help in country. Remember central issue of Reconstruction was the place of blacks in American life after slavery. Changing attitudes on this question strongly influenced later representations of the Reconstruction era, whether in historical writing or in the popular media. Indeed, what later generations imagined had happened in the South in the years immediately after the Civil War is a reliable index of how they viewed black and white relations in their own time.

During the 2000 a post revisionism began to develop. As it became apparent that the dream of equality for blacks was still unrealized, historians responded to the changing perceptions and complex cross-currents of black and white relations in their own time by taking another look at reconstruction. They will found, among other things, that those in change of efforts to make black and other races equal citizens in the 2000s had views that were quire moderate by the standards of the post civil rights era of the 1970s and 1980s. Black politicians, too, came in for critical reassessment. It was argued that many worked more for their own interests as members of a black middle class than for the kinds of policies such as land reform that would have met the vital needs of their impoverished constituents.

Some recent historians explain it in terms of an underlying racism that prevented white Republicans from identifying fully with the cause of black equality. Others stress the gulf between the class interests of those in charge of implementing and managing Reconstruction and the poor people of the South who were supposed to be its beneficiaries. The basic issue raised by Reconstruction how to achieve racial equality in America, has not yet been resolved. So long as this is the case, we will continue to look at our first effort in this direction for whatever guideposts it provides. We need to stop the hate of other races because Satan started it.

CHAPTER 3

Sinful Diseases

It should be noted first of all that the very use of the words "literature" or "book" in this connection may easily give rise to a serious misunderstanding, for these medical terms would seem to suggest that the God gave to the prophets were in the first instance literary figures. Both Old and New Testaments give much attention to bodily health in its relation to Christian faith. This is true also of the religions of Greece, Egypt, and Babylonia, and indeed of most primitive faiths. Generally, as can be seen in Homer, external injuries and affections were treated by common sense and often wise methods. But epidemics and obscurer complaints left the people helpless, and they had recourse to what seem to us superstitious Christian rites such as spells, processions, or magical mixtures. The history of the art and science of medicine has been largely the transfer of one type of ailment after another from treatment by superstitious or hit-and-miss methods to treatment by experimental knowledge. The general movement is typified by the shift in popular faith from solemn processions with sacred images in case of epidemics to modern methods of sanitation.

The shift has largely been a salutary one, but in the process something has been lost. Science says, "Whence proceeds the subtlest folly, but from the subtlest wisdom?" is really inscribed, though few scientist can see it, around the base of the image of the Lord God, which stands by the boulevard of modern life opposite Science. The two are different. They reign supreme, each over a section of human life. One must make friends with science to live at all. I once acknowledged that after I study religion, economic, and joined a organization order, given to it all my worldly possessions, and taken the wow of poverty, I found myself as much dependent upon the present evil economic system as ever. No matter how high in state, church, society or science the individual may be who makes pronouncement on any subject, the scientist always asks for the evidence.

When no evidence is produced other than personal dicta, past or present "Revelations" in dreams, or the "voice of God", the scientist can pay no attention whatsoever, except to ask.

How do they get that way? He or she is right as far as verifiable facts are concerned, but he or she forgets that the poetry and faith of today sometimes become the scientific fact of tomorrow, and that to live wisely man or woman has to make up his or her mind on more things than science can verify. We know very little about how things grow; we know more about disease than we do about health; there are strange powers of recovery in man and woman which Christian call God.

We can all help or hinder, but God does the growing in the garden and the healing in the hospital. Job 26:14 reads, "Lo, these are parts of his ways: but how little a portion is heard of him? But the thunder of his power who can understand?" Health is the continue maintenance of normal functioning of the human body under a favorable environment. It requires this favorable environment of temperature, moisture, air bacterial invasion and nutrition because it has developed to its present state of functioning by a long and gradual process of evolution and adaptation. And of course, health also presumes that there is a health body to start with.

However, the body's margin of adaptability is quite great, and it can maintain itself normally under most unfavorable conditions of invasion by bacteria and great variation of temperature and nutrition. But such conditions can be tolerated only to a certain limit, beyond which disease develops. The following diseases are identifiable in the Bible; these are some of the name of the diseases:

(1) Alcoholism is called strong drink cause intoxicating liquor. The Scripture by skekar; alcoholic beverages made from grapes are called yayin. There is evidence throughout Scripture that excessive drinking existed among rich and poor. Proverbs 23:30-31-31.

We who are Christians, we do not drink alcoholic beverages is so strong that he or she cannot control himself or herself. There is need to help people understand their feelings of inferiority and defeat, to help find more adequate ways of dealing with them. Some forms of escape mean only jumping from the frying pan into the fire. While the alcoholic can forget for a little time, he or she always comes back to face life again through eyes that are blurred with redness. A change in drinking habits can hardly occur unless such a man or woman has a change in his or her life philosophy.

The problems of alcoholism take on new dimensions in a machine age. The social consequence of drinking are more serious when the drinker is at the wheel of a fast-moving automobile, or when he or she is an engineer guiding a speeding streamlined train, or when he or she is a surgeon with a sharp instrument in his or her hand. The sage who insisted that rulers and clergyman should refrain from drinking wine saw that their position of repossibility made it necessary for them to have clear minds. They might too easily pervert justice if they were under the influence of alcohol. Today the number of those in positions where they can affect the lives of others is vastly increased.

The evil consequences of drunkenness do not fall on the drunken clergyman alone. The very lives of innocent people are jeopardized by those whose minds are darkened and whose reactions are impaired under the influence of alcohol. The problem of alcoholism is made more serious in nations where alcohol is sold for private profit. The distiller and the brewer must sell their products. They must try to produce consumers for their goods. Their aim is to make attractive the taking of strong drink. The resources of the printer's art and the advertising writer's cleverness are used to make drinking socially acceptable and the mark of a stalwart man or woman's accomplishments.

The Old Testament prophet would hardly be impressed by the modern presentation of portraits of users of alcohol. This is a business not for health of the individual. It may be a man or woman's business as to whether or not he or she wants to drink, but it ought not to be somebody's business to encourage him or her to drink in order to produce a profit for the alcohol merchant. Many young people are drinking alcoholic beverages. no single method has been able to solve this whole perplexing problem.

Prohibiting the sale of alcohol to young people or by law is not effective if there is no general disposition to support the law. Only as there is an under girding of a legal enactment by a community sentiment can law be effective in dealing with the small proportion of violators who might try to fly in the face of the wishes of a large majority.

The writer of this book in this chapter of regarding Proverbs seems to be advocating total abstinence. "Do not look at wine when it is red" verse 31. The best way to avoid the evil consequences of drinking too much is not to drink at all. Can you says that Jesus Christ drunk wine?

(2)   Blindness was often attributed to sin. A curse involving blindness as punishment for evil doing was superlative, as with the men or women of Sodom. The Bible speak of two types of blindness are mentioned in Scripture highly infectious ophthalmic, accentuated by dirt, dust, and glare, and blindness incident to old age, like that of Isaac in Gen. 27: 1, his Father Eli; I Sam 3:2, and Ahijiah in I Kings 14:4. Lev. 26:16 mentions blindness that results from malaria. Paul's temporary blindness along the Damascus way may have been amaurosis affecting the optic nerve in Acts 9:8. Old Testament prophet noted the pity felt for the blind, and recorded the prohibition against placing stumbling blocks in their way. A curse was invoked against those who willfully made the blind wander out of the way. Jesus in his peripatetic ministry was daily in intimate touch with afflicted blind sitting along the highways of Palestine, devoted much their stories dramatized many of his most urgent messages. To bring "recovering of sight to the blind" Luke 4:18-22 was one of the declared purposes of his anointment by the Lord. In these case reports three characteristics are notable.

(a)   The extraordinary cure was effected by the miraculous, positive therapeutics of Jesus Christ first hand touch with the afflicted.

(b)   Jesus Christ shunned spectacular acclaim by insisting that the cured should not "tell it to any in the town" in Mark 8:26, with one notable exception in Luke 7:22. © The cured were stirred by desire to follow their great benefactor immediately.

23

Sometimes their cure provoked heated attack by jealous Pharisees in John 9:15.

(3) Cancer or carcinoma is a malignant tumor or growth of various structure characteristics, which may develop in any tissue or organ and which may develop in any tissue or organ and which has a tendency to grow rapidly and beak up. When it breaks up, the fragments consisting of single cancer cells or groups of such cells are carried by the blood and lymph to different part of the body. In those days was Hezekiah sick unto death. And the prophet Isaiah the son Amoz came to him, and said unto him, "Thou said the Lord, Set thine house in order; for thou shalt die, and not live." The story of Hezekiah is a good example that prayer can change thing. Hezekiah's prayer is a noble expression of the sense of the frailty and brevity of life, of the awe and dread which a man or woman who has no hope of life beyond the grave must feel as he or she faces death. We can share in the mood of the dying Hezekiah, for we are one with him in our mortality; but the Christian has something which Hezekiah did not have, for between him and us stands the figure of Jesus Christ "who hath abolished death, and hath brought life and immortality to light" in II Timothy 1:10.

With graphic and imaginative power of Holy Spirit the author describes the scene in Hezekiah's chamber. Hezekiah sees the shadow of the sundial, on top of the courtyard steps, creeping slowly downward. Silent and inexorable it draws nearer, like the beckoning finger of death. In the mercy of God it was stayed and Hezekiah was spared. What any man or woman does with the life which is restored to him or her is always revealing. Hezekiah laid firmer grip on God, he made new discovery of the divine mercy and forgiveness, he saw deeper into the meaning and sacredness of life, and he rededicated himself of God.

This is the effect which every great sorrow and struggle has upon a noble soul. They bring back into time a sense of eternity. Note "Sorrow's subjects, they are our Hezekiah; wrestlers with death, our veterans; and to the rabble hordes of society they set the step of a nobler life. Read Ch. 39 reveals, Hezekiah did not remain true to his psalm of deliverance. There is always the danger that those who have come conquerors out of the struggle with death may fall a prey to common life. How awful to have fought for character with death only to squander it upon life. Then follows the difference that Jesus Christ has made to our meeting with death. Hezekiah had no sure faith in life beyond the grave. To him to die was to leave all his friends, even God himself. "I said I shall not see the Lord . . . in the land of the living; I shall behold man no more with the inhabitants of the world . . . They that go down into the pit cannot hope for thy truth" verse 11; 18. remember death for Hezekiah was postponed for fifteen years, but at the end of that respire lay the certainty of going out into darkness, and death would have the last word. He might face it with heroic resignation, but a faith that is good for this life alone, and not equal to the challenge of death, fails the soul at the crucial point. The author is point out more information concerned this subject. The subject deals with longtime sickness and death.

It is the glory of the Christian faith that it holds for all time and eternity. Jesus Christ has taken the measure of sin and death, and is therefore able to save unto the uttermost. Because of his victory and his love we are persuaded that not even death "shall be able to separate us from the love of God" Romans 8:38-39. That faith has transfigured life for untold multitudes who have faced death clear-eyed and unafraid because of their trust in their Jesus Christ and Savior. This is the secret of the peaceful hearts, the unfaltering spirit of those who were persuaded that Christ was able to keep that which they committed unto him against the day of death.

The account of Hezekiah's mortal sickness is told with great vividness and detail in II Kings 20:1-11, a passage which stands as an illustration of the superb narrative power of Hebrew genius. Our chapter, however, is enriched by the inclusion of Hezekiah's prayer of thanksgiving on his recovery. There is here a wealth of material for the interpreter. We are confronted throughout with the solemn question, "What is a man or woman's hope as he or she faces death?"

Considering that no one can escape, it is the more strange that men and women so generally refuse to face that last sure fact.

They are reluctant to think about it, much less talk about it. Yet probably the final revelation of man or woman's character, his or her courage, his or her faith, is the way in which he or she meets it. Why should we be so unwilling to entertain the idea of dying, when it is the one experience common to the race?

We need not become morbidly concerned about it. Morbidity is always unhealthy. But surely it would be a natural thing, and the part of wisdom, so to prepare ourselves for the great adventure that we could contemplate it with dignity and without fear. No man or woman has thought his or her way through the implications of his or her faith till he or she has made quite clear to himself or herself what his or her hope is when he or she looks toward that last threshold. The good impression left on the mind of a Christian when he or she reads this story of Hezekiah is the awesomeness of the thought that death is the end of everything.

Unconsciously, and without considering its full import, the modern generation has largely taken for granted the Christian faith in immortality. Therefore to read of a man or woman facing death, convinced that there is nothing beyond it, brings us up short. It brings into focus the amazing difference that the Christian faith makes. The ancient Hebrews saw no reason to believe in immortality; neither could they ignore it.

Their conception of Sheol was, as it were, a compromise between the idea of extinction and the idea of life after death. They died and were ushered from the warm, rich contacts of life into an unsubstantial and meaningless existence. Death meant the end of anything that could be called life. The dead had no employment, no real fellowship, and worst of all, and have touch with God. It was says by the Hebrew saying goodby to God, which to the Hebrew invested death with terror. They were not afraid to die, but they shrank from the thought of separation from God. Sheol was not a place of torment; its horror consisted in the fact that the soul was but a shadow of itself.

To us it is an unbearable thought that all the goodness and truth for which we have striven, all the fair hopes which we have cherished, and above all, those dear souls we have loved, should be blotted out eternally lost to us through death. The native courage of the human heart is nowhere more clearly shown than in those countless generations who faced life, and died valiantly, without any hope beyond the grave. It is no wonder that through the ages certain elect of the race have protested against the finality of death, and in the face of received tradition have flung out their surmise that it will not have the last word. Against all the evidence, without a vestige of proof, heroic souls have denied the omnipotence of death, daring to declare their unsupported conviction that there must be life beyond. That was the deduction of faith; their trust in God made it a necessity.

Brave as it was, however, it had no confirmation till Jesus Christ "brought life and immortality to light" II Tim. 1:10. Even yet, with his victory and his word, belief in eternal life is always a matter of faith. It is what the writer of Hebrews calls "the assurance of things hoped for" Heb. 11:1. We Christian has no proof, as such of immortality; he or she can only say in the presence of death, like St. Paul in Romans 8:38-39 says, "For I am persuaded, that neither dearth, nor life, nor angels, nor principalities, nor powers, nor things present, nor things to come. Nor, height, nor depth, nor any other creature, shall be able to separate us from the love of God, which is in Christ Jesus our Lord". We who are Christian believe is Jesus Christ words, Jesus said, "In my Father's house are many mansions: if it were not so, I would have told you. I go to prepare a place for you. And if I go and prepare a place for you, I will come again, and receive you unto myself; that where I am, there ye may be also". John 14:2-3 It is enough. It is better than proof; it is the promise word of our Jesus Christ. The great hope has become his promise. Of all the world Christians alone has a fact on which to rest its assurance of eternal life: the fact of Jesus Christ victory over death, and the truth that "God so loved the world, that he gave his only begotten Son, that whosoever believeth in him should not perish, but have everlasting life". John 3:16. There the matter rests. We know the love that will not let us go. It is to that love we give our dear ones when they die; it is into our Father's hands that we commend our spirit as we ourselves launch out into death.

In that faith untold multitudes have died triumphantly; the waters of death have been shallow to their feet because of their trust in Jesus Christ. Eternal life, what that means no man or woman can say. Our Lord Jesus Christ was silent on the conditions of life in the many mansions of God. It is as if He said, as we say to our children about some great surprise, "Wait and see". In the meantime, nothing can keep us from wondering about it. Surely we have authority to let loose our imagination and see with the eyes of faith the condition and employment of out loved ones in that other country, with that great company of the redeemed which no man or woman can number.

None can deny us that right; and though we have nothing to guide our thoughts but love, and in a sense all our speculations are vain, yet it not only bring comfort to our spirit just to talk about that place of peace, it also quickens our expectations of the best which is yet to be. And when we have done, when the gates of the heavenly city swing to, shutting from our longing eyes all the glory and the wonder, there comes to us this word, "Eye hath not seen, nor ear heard, neither have entered into the heart of man, the things which God hath prepared for them that love him: I Cor. 2: 9.

There are many verses in the Bible concerning this subject, which open our vistas of truth. Some says on their sick bed, "What shall I say? Will he spoken unto me, will he do it; I shall go softly all my years in the bitterness of my soul". When you are face long sick or death, some says, I shall go softly, they say; and it means with humility, because of the things learned in bitter hours. A man or woman has not suffered in vain if he or her can carry into all that life shall thereafter hold for him or her a sense of the littleness of time and the greatness of eternity. II Chronicles 21:18, and Leviticus 26:16.

(4) Cutaneous disease affecting the skin. Skin diseases were prominently associated with Egypt in Deut. 28:27-35. In the previous plague all the cattle had died. If these accounts were to be understood as a sober recital of fact, it would be difficult to know what beast was left to suffer this disease. Cutaneous diseases associated with boils, tumors, itch, and sores in Exodus 9:9; Leviticus 13:18; Deut. 28:27-30; II Kings 20:7; and Isaiah 1:6.

This associated with leprosy, a white or reddish white spot may appear different with people, where the boil was, and if it is sunk in the skin, and the hair upon it is turned white, leprosy is to be diagnosed. If these symptoms are absent, the person shall be put in quarantine for a week and then prounced clean if there is no spreading of the inflammation. You should notice that the subject is associated with the curses is parallel to that come with a blessings. Every curses of the individual life shall be accursed if he or she and his or her nation are disloyal to God. Whatever he or she does will fail, and nature will be aligned against him or her. The first portion details the blessing that follow upon the challenge. If you obey the voice of the Lord God all these blessings shall come upon you. Reads Deut. 28:1-2. The other part is concerned with the curses that follow upon disobedience, If you will not obey the voice of the Lord God, all these curses shall come upon you, verse 15.

(5)   Dropsy is an abnormal accumulation of fluid in the tissues and body cavities due mostly to a disturbance in the blood circulation, in the condition of the smallest arteries as(capillaries)and in the body chemistry as ca result of heart, liver or kidney disease. Each one of the first and second trios just mentioned seems to complicate and drag in the rest, so that in the end the complete sextet is often present to plague the poor human body. Parent with dropsy are given a balanced daily diet nowadays of all foods excepting those mentioned in the Bible that Jesus Christ heal them. If you are know spiritual heal your doctor will put you on a diet, and are even permitted to take enough liquid, but their diet must be salt-free and sodium-free. Cook and prepare all foods without salt, do not eat any pickled, smoked or salted meat or fish, no bread, crackers and butter prepared with salt, and no caviar, clams, oysters, peanut-butter, condensed milk, cheese, carrots, cowpeas, spinach, endive, olives or raisins. You may eat the following foods once a week with your doctor order. Buttermilk, lima beans, beets, cantaloupe, cauliflower, celery, chard, cocoanut, currants, dates, figs, melons, peanuts, peaches, pumpkin, radish, rutabaga, strawberries, turnip and watercress. Luke 14:2-3 reads, "And, behold, there was a certain man before him which had the

dropsy. And Jesus answering spake unto the lawyers and Pharisees, saying, Is it lawful to heal on the Sabbath day?"

(6) Dumbness lacking the power of speech; mute or unwilling to talk. Matt. 9:32-33 reads, "As they went out, behold, they brought to him a dumb man possessed with a devil. And when devil was cast out, the dumb spake: and the multitudes marveled, saying, It was never so seen in Israel".

(7) Dysentery any of various intestinal inflammations characterized by abdominal pain and intense diarrhea with bloody. II Chronicles 21:15 that Elijah warned Ahab and Jezebel about themselves will have a severe sickness with a disease of your bowels, until your bowels come out because of the disease, day by day. This disease is an inflammation of the intestine characterized by fever, abdominal pains, ulcerations of the bowel, vomiting and diarrhea with bloody stools. This disease is caused by germs, worms or viruses, and depending on the cause it is variously called bacillary, amebic, giardiac and virus dysentery. Contact your doctor if you experience fever, abdominal pains, weakness, and bloody stools. God can heal you with his Spiritual healing power in Acts 28:8.

(8) Endocine disturbances is any gland producing one or more internal sections that are introduced directly into the bloodstream and carried to other parts of the body whose functions they regulate or control. They act in unison and harmony with each other, in their common purpose of controlling, coordinating, and stimulating all vital body functions, such as secretion, metabolism, growth, and reproduction. Leviticus 21:20; I Sam 17:14.

(9) Epilepsy is a chronic disease of the nervous system. This is a disease which has been known to mankind since ancient times, but is as yet one of the many unsolved puzzles of medicine. Some doctors think it is not a disease entity, but only a symptom of an underlying condition which we fail to understand. Many disease of childhood, as, for instance, scarlet fever and pneumonia, often start with convulsions, but the convulsion is only a symptom of the oncoming disease. In epilepsy there might be a systemic

upset, chemical hormonal or nervous in character, which when understood may likely be possible to control. What doctors call epilepsy is an epileptic state following severe injury to the head and causing adhesions in the skull. Matt. 17:15.

(10) Eye disease is xanthelasma are somewhat elevated, yellow deposits in the skin of the lids. They have the color of yellow butter or yellow chamois, and are the result of excessive (cholesterol) formation and retention in the body. They are often caused by an excessive intake of fatty food and by some defect in the fat digestion. It is the same material which gets deposited in the walls of the blood vessels causing arterisclerosis. This condition usually occurs in middle aged people. Don't wait long when these deposits begin to appear on the eyelids or other parts. Gen. 27:1; Gen. 29:17;and Proverbs 23:29.

(11) Fever is the rise of body temperature above the normal 98.6 F. more fever are due to infectious disease, infections in any part of the body virus infections and great mental upsets. When a fever lasts longer than two weeks, it is mostly due to tuberculosis or a pus infection in some part of the body. The symptoms accompanying any fever are headache, aches all over the body, exhaustion, flushed face, hot, dry skin, loss of appetite, nausea or vomiting, constipation or diarrhea, restlessness, rapid pulse and respiration, and highly concentrated, deep colored urine. Luke 4:38 reads,

> "and he rose out of the synagogue, and entered into Simons house. And Simon's wife's mother was taken with a great fever; and they besought him for her".

(12) Gonorrhea is an acute, contagious venereal disease most commonly contracted through sexual intercourse, mostly promiscuous. We find from history that since World War II, and other wars with the demoralized conditions wars bring about, it happens now and then that a young man and young woman will contract gonorrhea from his wife and her husband. Of course, when a husband or wife infects his or her partner, as often happened formerly before

the war, that is nothing to bag about either. Both instance could and should be prevented under all conditions. No one having an uncured gonorrheal condition has a right to be married until he or she is entirely free of the disease. There are about 1,000,000 new gonorrheal infections yearly in the United States America. The infection occurs among the younger age groups. The age limits among males are 17 to 45 and among females 17 to 30. We need to educated young people about this disease. God can heal you from this disease. Gen. 20:17 Reads, "So Abraham prayed unto God: and God healed A-bime-lech, and his wife, and his maidservants; and they bare children.

(13) Gout is said to be a disease of the well-to-do, and of the overfed, also of those indulge in alcoholic liquors, and especially in the fermented beer or wines. Certainly, if the sons and daughters indulge in the same table pleasures as the father, they will suffer the same consequences because of the inheritance of the good fortune and the abundance of larder and table luxury. The chief trouble in gout is a retention of urid in the system. Uric acid is a product of protein metabolism, and is normally excreted by the kidney's; but in gout it accumulates in the blood, from where it gets deposited in the skin and joints, and may also form gravel and stones in the kidneys. II Chronicles 16:12.

(14) Lameness disqualified a man from becoming a priest of yahweh. Lame is a crippled or disabled; having an injured leg or foot that makes one limp. Jesus Christ disciples effected miraculous cures of the lame, Peter and John in the Temple in Acts 3:2-13.; Philip in Samaria in Acts 8:7.

(15) Leprosy is an infectious disease, but it does not seem to be (catching) like other contagious diseases. The Bible give a different meaning. Leprosy is a chronic infectious disease, constantly present in the tropics and parts of the orient. True leprosy in its symptoms is, of all diseases, one of the most horrible to the onlooker. To the natural repulsion which it evokes there was added for the Hebrew the sense that it was a defilement under the law. And there came a leper to him, beseeching him, and kneeling down to him, and

saying unto him, If thou wilt, thou canst make clean. And Jesus Christ, moved with compassion, put forth his hand, and touched him, and saith unto him, I will; be thou clean". Mark 1:40-41. Jesus Christ touching of the leper was a breach of the law. It was also a supreme illustration of the gospel in action. In India the Brabmans are a people apart, polluted by the touch or even the shadow of an outcaste man; yet there, in a leper hospital, was once a devoted superintendent, a Brahman by birth, a Christian by conversion. It is not given to man or woman to see a more signal illustration of the power of the gospel patient is clean. It is thought that the reference here may be to common white leprosy, as distinguished from the malignant varieties. Exodus 4:6; Lev. 13:1-17; Numbers 12:10-11; and II Kings 7:3.

(16) Mental disorders is report that a virus or germ of such a common infection as rheumatism may invade the arteries of the brain and give rise to the mental illness psychiatrists cell by the cabalistic name schizophrenia. Mentally ill person are sick people and very often the so called mental symptoms are merely manifestations of a disease in some part of the body or the brain itself, just as the delirium and mental derangement of the typhoid, pneumonia, scarlet fever or meningitis person is only a minor part of the general picture of the original disease. I Sam 21:13; II Thessalonians 3:6-7; II Thessalonians 3:11.

(17) Malaria is a parasitic disease cause by the plasmodium of which there are several varieties. The parasite is carried by mosquitoes (Genus Anopheles) and transmitted by its bite, sucking it up from an infected person's blood and injecting it into a healthy person. We find that the best way to prevent the disease is to dry up or drain or fill in all swamp land near dwelling places, remove everything that retains water, such as old buckets, water barrels, cans and bottles, keep weeds and grass cut low around homes, screen doors and windows. You need to know, malarial attacks develop a week or two after exposure, after being bitten by the anopheles mosquito. They start with a severe chill, violent shaking, shivering and chattering of the teeth. After half an hour comes the fever stage. There are now other drugs than quinine

for the treatment of malaria, such as Atabrine and Plasmochin, but quinine is still the stand by. St Paul said II Corinthian 12:7 reads, "And least I should be exalted above measure through the abundance of the revelations, there was given to me a thorn in the flesh, the messenger of Satan to buffet me, lest I should be exalted above measure.

(18) Paralysis is loss of sensation and motion in a part of the body is termed paralysis. Paralysis may be of prenatal origin or it may be cause by injury to nerves during birth. Injuries during later life, infections, pressure of tumors, meningitis, brain hemorrhage, and metallic poisons may result in paralysis. This disease affected infants and it may attack adult as well.

Also, paralysis is not always a complication or consequence of this disease. Most peoples affected never show signs of paralysis, and of those who do show some degree of paralysis the great majority recover their normal use of all muscles. II Sam. 4:4; Matt. 4:24; Mark. 2:3-5; and Matt. 12:10.

(19) Pestilence or Bubonic Plaque is a fatal infection characterized by the appearance of enlarged, painful lymphatic glands (buboes) attaining the size of a walnut. If confined to one part of the body, the course of the disease may be mild. But it commonly spreads and attacks other parts, bringing on pneumonia or blood poisoning (septicemia). There are two types of Buboes. Buboes of this kind must not be confused with buboes caused by veneral disease. This disease often starts with servere chills followed by high fever, aches and pains all over the body, headache, delirium, puffy face and inflamed eyes. In some cases, coma and death in a few days follow the delirium. The cause of bubonic plague is the Bacillus pest carried by infected rats transmit it to fleas, who in turn bite men, or women, or child, thus transmitting this horrible pest to the choice of creation. The flea bites the rat and gets a stomach of rat's blood filled with plague germs. When it bites the man or woman or child, the flea finds this extra mouthful too much, so it evacuates and vomits its gastro-intestinal contents contents loaded with the germ right there and then. The man

or woman feeling the itch of the lea's bite, starts scratching like nobody's business. He or she thus inoculates himself or herself thoroughly with the germs of the excreta the flea left behind. In a few days (3 to 10) the bitten man or woman or child is prostrated with the dread disease. As you may or may not know, that a man or woman who knows what is good for him or her should have no rats or nice around. Jeremiah 21:6 reads, "And I will smite the inhabitants of this city, both man and beast: they shall die of a great pestilence. Ezekiel 6:11-12.

(20) This continual on Plagues, the Scripture to indicate: (a) an affliction or calamity viewed as a visitation from God. There are Ten Plagues of Egypt. (b) a pestilence or epidemic of high mortality, such as afflicted the Philistines after their capture of the Ark. Possibly Bubonic plague, or the pestilence that followed David's census, or the one threatened in the reign of Judah's King Jehoram. © any tormenting situation diease or otherwise as in Psalms 9:10 reads, "Neither shall any plague come nigh thy dwelling". The first mention of a diease plague visited on an individual and his family is that suffered by Pharaoh because of Sarah, wife of Adraham.

Who had been represented to the King as Abraham's sister. This may be early record of venereal disease. Plagues were feared as penalties for disobedience to God's laws. The Ten Plagues of as follows:

(1) The Nile waters are turned to blood, Abyssinian red siol come down the Nile as it rises to flood, and makes the stream appear very red a situation associated by Egyptians with a period of cures. The Egyptians promised nothing after the first plague, because they were able to reproducr it themselves. The effect of the next plagues is greater and, in order to get rid of them, Pharaoh promises to let the people go. But as soon as the scare is over, he cannot bring himself to keep his promise. (2) Frogs breed as flood water recedes. Birds such as the ibex usually keep them in check, but in this instance the flogs kept

on multiplying. After the second plague (frogs) he simply refuses to keep his promise.

After the other plagues he shifts his ground.

(3) Gnate or Lice or mosquitoes, swarms of these bloodsuckers attack men and beasts in the fall field of Egypt. The third plague (vermin) forces him to give the people the right to sacrifice to their God, but inside the land of Egypt. Moses rejects this compromise on the ground that the sacrificial ceremonies of the Hebrews would be so different from those of the Egyptians as to cause bigoted riots among the Egyptians.

(4) Files or dog flies possibly the tsetse fly. The result of the fouth plague (pestilence) was that Pharaoh said they could go, but not as far from the border as they desired. But Moses holds to his requisite of three day's journey.

(5) Cattle murrain, spread by decomposing bodies of grogs from which bacteria were carried by flies. The announcement of the plague is again conditional. But this time Pharaoh receives a brief twenty-four hour unltimatum. It is impossible to specify the disease that constitutes the plague; the common view that it was anthrax is not demonstrable. All the cattle were struck, include camels among others. The reference to camels in thirteenth century Egypt seems anachronistic, for it is not likely that this animal was domesticated in Egypt as early as that time. In the thirteenth century B.C. the domestication of the camel had not yet progressed to a point where it could have any decisive effect upon nomadism; no traces of domestic camels have been yet discovered in any contemporary record or excavation. It is until the eleventh century that camel riding nomads first appear in our documentary sources. Notice that Pharaoh notices the sign of God's in the exemption of Israel, but remains unmoved.

(6) Boils on man and beast, plague boils, which in Egypt often cause great mortally. Moses performs the wonder in Pharaoh's presence and a form of magical action of the sympathetic type relpaces the use of the miraculous rod. The nature of this plague is reminiscent of the one preceding it. However, author felt that the fine dust over all the land point to the darkness of the ninth plague. Some sort of malignant pustule constituted the plague. Skin disease were prominently associated with Egypt in Deut. 28:29-35. In the previous plague all the cattle had died. If these accounts were to be understood as a sober recital of fact, it would be difficult to know what beast was left to suffer this disease. The magicians had already given up the struggle against God's. Now they can no longer protect even themselves. The contest moves on to the full victory of the Lord God.

(7) Hail a rare occurrence in Egypt. The seventh plague of hail brings the further concession on the part of Pharaoh that the men could go, but no one else. Moses rejects this suggestion, as the sacrifice requires the presence of all.

(8) Locusts always a bane of the Middle East. Pharaoh, after the eight (locusts), goes a little further and permit men, women, and children to go, but would keep their flocks and herds in Egypt; Moses answers that this would enrage God's more than anything, as the flocks and herds are needed for the sacrifice. Thus everything is now ready for Moses to play his trump cared, and proclaim the eighth plague which will free the people. Before Moses use of the rod to bring the plague, and the conclusion is. After Moses has warned Pharaoh of the coming plague, and before it strikes, some of the court nobles compel the ruler to recall Moses for the purpose of arbitrating the conflict, but this inevitably fails since in a struggle with God for lordship a true is unthinkable.

He alone is God. But this attempt at negotiation before a plague strikes is a new feature in this series of accounts. After the plague has come Pharaoh, as usual sends for Moses to ask him to intercede. But here an attempt at negotiation is conspicuously absent. One inevitably gets the feeling that this characteristic bit of must have been transferred to some other location. Is it perhaps the interview that now precedes the actual coming of the plague?

Or is it, as author suggests, the account of the interview that now forms a part of the next two plagues. That interview, which ends in a violent scene at which Pharaoh sentences Moses series of plagues leading up to the death of the first born. It show unmistakably the hand of God and seems to fit the note of finality introduced by Pharaoh, where he asks for forgiveness only this once. It is also strange that in its present position this interview of Moses with Pharaoh, in which the latter offers concessions, is not accompanied by his request for Moses intercession to stop the plague.

Previously such a request occurs without the offer of concessions as a bribe. This is a strong argument for transferring these verses to the account of the eighth plague. Such a transfer reduces the next plague to a mere skeleton, all from man and beast. This is a strong argument today about "locusts". One swarm of locusts which crossed the Red Sea in 1889 was estimated to be two thousand square miles in extent. In Cyprus in 1881 official reports state that 1,300 tons of locust eggs were destroyed. Swarms have been seen at sea 1,200 miles from land. The Arabs today are losers every year by swarms bred in the land or carried to them by winds. They wrap the spring clusters of dates around with wisps of dry foliage for protection, and afterward avenge themselves on the ravenous hordes by beating down the insects with palm braches, then toasting, and eating history stated.

(9) Darkness such as occurs when the blighting, wind, burns and blinds with dust. The plague here differs from the other plagues. There are no divine instructions, no interview with Pharaoh. Very early in the study of the text, even when the Greek translation of the Hebrew was made, this darkness was connected with khamsin, the wind that blows in the spring and brings with it clouds of sand and dust, darkening the

sun. For a poetical description of it for the Egyptians this terror would be the more frightful because they believed that evil spirits were abroad in the darkness.

For well the Egyptians deserve to be deprived of light and imprisoned by darkness; they who had kept in close ward thy sons, through whom the incorruptible light of the law was to be given to the race of men.

(10) Death of the Egyptian first born, the climax of all the other plagues. Ever since the plagues led to Israel's escape their story has repeated in the Haggadah read at every Passover Seder. In every home in Egypt at midnight the eldest son dies, from the heir apparent in the king's palace to the son of the wretched felon in the cell in Exodus 12:29; the poor maid sitting grinding corn behind the hand mill loses her boy too in Exodus 11:5. As in Matt. 2:18, there was "In Rama was there a voice heard, lamentation, and weeping, anf great mourning, Rachel weeping for her children, and would not be comforted, because they are not". It was a night of horror. Pharaoh rose up, he, and all his servants, and all Egyptians and there was a great cry in Egypt: for there was not a house where there was not one dead in Exodus 12:30.

Then Moses was sent for and, without conditions, was granted everything he had asked. The wonderful picture he had painted for the people's imagination by his faith in God had actually come true. Everything was done to get the now unwelcome guests out of Egypt as soon as possible. Costly gifts were pressed upon them, if only they would leave at once; for the Egyptians were urgent upon the people, to send them out of the land in haste. In spite of the plagues God's bless them though the plagues. Read Exodus 12:1-20, but verse 1 and 2, "And the Lord spake unto Moses and Aaron in the land of Egypt, saying, This month shall be unto you the beginning of months: it shall be first month of the year to you". We find the writer here represents the people as absolutely unprepared for the sudden realization of all their hopes. They were not ready for a journey.

They had to take the dough which they had set out in the evening for bread before it was leavened; and on the way they had to bake matzoth mean "flat thin unleavened bread". So we have seen the strokes of God strike like lightning, each bolt more terrifying than the last. We have held our breath each time to see if Pharaoh will not yield to the inevitable. Now at last, long after his advisers had seen his case was hopeless, Pharaoh capitulated. The great duel between Pharaoh and Moses was over, and Moses had won. Remember Pharaoh had everything armies of soldiers, cities filled with treasure, a rich land; Moses on the other hand had nothing but a disorganized gang of slaves, and God on his side. But it is better to have nothing and God on one's side than to have everything except God.

In spite of all the tragedy in Egypt, it was a great day for the lonely man who had communed with his God in solitary prayer, who had to go on in spite of the discontent and murmuring of his own people, who had seen one attempt after another fail, who had at times even doubted if God had treated him fairly. I'm reminded of the words I reader of Woodrow Wilson, who knew all about the loneliness of leadership, at the dedication in 1916 of the memorial built over the log cabin birthplace in Hodgensville, Kentucky, the Lincoln home. For the clergyman leader of today, it is well to remember the secret toil which is the price of public leadership. People today should remember this may be early record of venereal disease. Plagues were feared as penalties for disobedience to God's laws.

(21) Sun-Stroke or Heat Prostration or Heat Stoke. Heat prostration is a condition affecting overworked and weak individuals when overheated. The person turns pale, the skin is cool and clammy, they are dizzy and faint, and may be nauseous and vomit. Heat stroke is the result of direct over exposure to the hot summer sun. The skin is red hot, the person feels dizzy, faint, nauseous, has ringing in the ears, sees spots before they eyes and may run a very

high temperature. Place him or her in a cool room, remove his or her clothing, sponge him or her with cool water and give him or her cool drinks but no stimulants. II Kings 4:18-35, this story is a beautiful one from beginning to end.

It is full of grace and charm. We find that the inmitial kindness of the woman and her husband was in no expectation of any reward but was the spontaneous expression of hospitable hearts. It was not she who asked anything in return from Elisha. It was he who inquired of his servant Gehazi what he could do for her. There followed the gift of a child and the child's restoration to life after he had Sun Stroke and died. Poignant is the story of the woman's grief. We are told that she was a wealthy woman. but grief spares none, high or low.

The community of suffering makes the whole world relatives. She insisted on going in person to Elisha. She had learned to believe in and trust the man whose power she had begun to know. Perhaps on of the greatest rewards of any "man of God" today is to win the faith and coinfidence of person in need. Thus is described to us the reciprocal relation of two noble persons. The woman's native sympathy and kindness had caused her to entertain an angel unawares. So, often in person experience a casual gesture of kindness, the simple expression of good will and sympathy, brings in its train rich rewards, unexpected blessing.

Elisha, too, might have accepted what was offered him as only what was dur to a man of God. Not so. What could he do to requite this kindness? At once is revealed the heart of any true "man of God". Inquiry disclosed the woman's secret want. How often under the external appearance of prosperity and well being there lies the hidden disappointment. To detect this and to seek to satisfy the hungry soul is one of the finest ministries of any "man of God".

Some ask the questions, did Elisha really restore to life the son of the Shunammite woman? If so, it loses none of its spiritual significance. For in verse 34, we are given a graphic description of what it costs to bring the dead to life. Only life can restore life. Only the uttermost giving of self can breathe the breath of life into the otherwise dead. Only the stretching of one's soul upon the soul of one out of which all semblance of life has vanished can quicken it again. It was by Jesus Christ stretching of himself upon the cross of his infinite sacrifice that he brought to life again men and women that were dead in their trespasses and sins.

(22) Worms is larvae of insects which eat organic matter, like bread, or wool, or the human body, and vegetable. Before I go any further, let me remind the reader of what was emphasized in worms; that most worm infestations are not just mere nuisances but are the cause of most serious and complicated chronic conditions of ill health and the cause of premature dear. I thank the God's we have no more worm infections than the number of our population. But it has recently been estimated that one in every three Americans is worm infected. The preventive treatment of worms is of course the most important.

Because the curative treatment will never catch up with the number of people as long as the means and sources of infection are not cut off. And prevention resolves itself into: (1) Securing a pure and sanitary water supply for all peoples. (2) Cooking for at least 30 minutes of all fish, pork, ham, and their products before eating, and cooking all other suspected foods. (3) Good personal hygiene. Twenty thousand of our military of the Pacific, and over sea have been infected with the "filariasis" worm.

The people in tropical and subtropical countries are mostly infested with worms. Many people in these parts of the world are infested with five or more types of worms all because of poor hygiene and sanitation, and contaminated water supplies. So when you travel in South America, India, Asia or Africa take the greatest precaution about your food and water. But let us get back to our own country lest we be told to remove a beam from our own eye. And we certainly have more that a "mote in our eye" to contend with. Before I go any further, let me remind the reader of what was emphasized in several topics in this book.

In our country it has recently been estimated that one in every five Americans is worm infected; we have about 31,000,000 citizens infested with hog-worms, trichinosis; at least 3,500,000 are infested with hook-worms, and twenty thousands are infested with tapeworms, pinworms and roundworms. A recent survey of all the school children of a prosperous and enlightened Eastern town proved that 30% of these children were infested with some one or another type of worm. This is not a mote in the eye; it is a bolt and a brickbat between our eyes and it is high time we woke up, sat up and took notice of the twenty of millions of trichinosis cases all over the country, of more than a million hookworm cases in South and all the other worm gnawing at our entrails and at our very marrow.

The preventive treatment of worms is of course the most important. Because the curative treatment will never catch up with the number of cases as long as the means and sources of infection are not cut off. But we have treatment to fight against the worm and infection. Larvae of insects which eat organic matter, like bread in Exodus 16:24 or wool in Isaiah 51:8; vegetable matter in Jonah 4:7; or the human body in Job 19:26; and 21:26. The cause of this disease of follows: (1) Sin of the individual, punished by God. (2) Son of parents. (3) Seduction by Satan some suggest that there is explanation for diseases.

The Mosaic law forbidding the touching of the dead prevented postmortem study of anatomy and causes of disease. But many sensible laws of hygiene and sanitation contributed to the prevention of disease, as concerning sex life. Sin is essentially a Christian idea; it always presupposes God determines what regard as sinful. Always in the Bible teaching sin has a God reference. Men and women are sinners because they have gone contrary to the will of God, or to what they took his will to be, or to what they might have known his will to be. This rebelliousness is charged to all; there is none Jewish and the Christian faith can do.

Sin, however, goes deeper than the will; it is primarily a matter of the heart. The sinful deed expresses a still deeper sinfulness and the problem lies with that deeper sinfulness. That is, with the natural disposition. There is in the Bible, however, recognition not only of individual sin but of corporate or general sin as well. There is a procedure known as Thrombocytopenia (ITP). This cause the blood cells known as platelets play a vital part in the mechansims of the body that stop bleeding. If you have Thrombocytopenia (ITP), your blood contains about one-third or less of the normal number of platelets. As a result, blood longer than is normal if you are injured of if you begin to bleed internally or externally for any reason. We find, this usually caused by the body forming antibodies, normally protective biochemicals; that attack its own platelets. Healthy platelets are damaged and then removed from the bloodstream at a high rate. This is known as acute (ITP), which stands for immune Thrombocytopenia purpura; its cause is unknown. It may also occur because of a medicine you are taking for an unrelated purpose. In some cases, it occurs relatively often in people who are receiving known as(Radiation Therapy or Chemtherapy for cancer).

Thrombocytopenia can occur as a symptom of other blood disorders such as Leukemia your platelet count can reduced when you age given many blood transfusions in a short period of time, during major surgery, for example, or when abnormal bleeding and clotting occur with another disorder. This condition of thrombocytopenia is a rash that consists of minute, bright red and dark red dots. These dots are actually tiny areas of bleeding in your skin. The rash can appear on any part of your body, but it often begins on the legs and wherever your skin has been irritated. After review all the medical information, we find that you can be treated immediately; if you notice the characteristic rash or any other abnormal bleeding.

Yours physician will probably review all medicines you may be taking for another disorder; and will take a blood sample for laboratory analsis. The blood test will show the platelet level, and indicate whether the thrombocytopenia is a sign of another disease. Some physician, usually a bone marrow examination is required to determine if platelets are being made in the marrow. They probably stop most or all medicine you may be taking, because virtually any medicine can produce thrombocytopenia. If the cause appears to be an antibody, your physician my prescribe a medicine known as (Sleroid), medicine to decrease the destruction cause by antibodies.

This will allow the level of platelets in your blood to rise. The disease often improves or disappears often a few weeks. If it doesn't your physician may advise you to have a (Splenectomy), an operation in which your spleen is removed. The spleen normally destroys worn out red cells, but it can become enlarged, and overactive, in some cases. If this occurs, the spleen may also destroy platelets, and prevent you from recovering quickly.

If you have thrombocytopenia that is caused by underproduction of platelets by the bone marrow or by blood less caused by bleeding or abnormal clotting, you may need transfusions of platelets. The unit is known as Cobe Spector (ITP), flow Path, the Plasmaphersis is a procedure in which blood is removed from the vein and spun in a centrifuge to separate plasma from blood cells. The cells, along with replacement plasma, are then reinjected into the person's vein. Plasmaphersis takes about two hours or more, apart from the discomfort of insertion of needles into veins, in virtually painless. The author was a dead man. In fact, he was officially declared with a deadly disease. At 8:oo p.m. in Pensacola, Florida Seaced Heart hospital emergency room. Dr. Sherlock a disease specialist was attending to his patient when he was summoned to the ER, but he knew his presence on the scene was not only a last resort but also most likely a lost cause.

The author blood was less than 5% percent, and his platelets was 5% percent, and his heart stop a full 60 minutes had come and gone since his heart beat last. His pupils were fixed and dilated, he'd been down too long. By the time the author arrived at the emergency room, author platelets had already been less rhan 5% percent. Just to make sure, Dr. Sherlock gave the author rounds of medications and other efforts had all failed to revive him.

The author lips, fingers, and toes had literally stop moving with unconscious from a lack of blood and oxygen. They said, there was no doubt the author was dead. After author unconscious, nearly everyone left the room. Nobody was left in the room and specter of unconscious. While Dr. Sherlock prepared to talk author wife, the nurse prepared author life-less body for the morgue, Dr. Sherlock remained in the room to write up his final report.

Then, once he complete his paperwork, Dr. Sherlock headed toward the door to talk to the author wife regarding her husband unconscious condition. Standing in the door's threshold, however, he was overcome with a strong feeling. A deep-seated sense that God wanted him to turn around and see the author hands move.

At first, Dr. Sherlock a man of science was somewhat reluctant, not embarrassed. But the request from author before his arrived at the emergency room he prayer to God that he will be healed and the condition was nothing.

And even through the author prayer before going to the emergency room, he prayer the pray: The God of Abraham, The God of Isaac, The God of Jacob; hear my prayer, I am your servants standing in the need of pray. I'm have pain in my chest, and I am going to the emergency room, go with me. God's help the doctors to remove this pain in my chest. If it your will, let it be done. In Jesus name we pray." Amen. Then the strange thing happened. The author head move, and his right arm shot up in a gesture of prayer and praise. At that moment, Dr. Sherlock inform author wife that he is alive. Dr. Sherlock order treated immediately contact Dr. German Herrera to given author transfusion to replace the platelets. Because author platelets was less of the normal number. Dr. Herrera injected into the author vein and spun in a centrifuge to separate plasma from blood cells. The cells, along with replacement plasma are then reinjected into the author vein. It takes about four hours or more, apart from the comfort of insertion of needles into veins and it painless. The author after the diagnosis, Dr. Herrera cut down author medicine, and author believe that Dr. German Herrera learn that God's and science can work together. The author learn more about the treatment of Thrombocytopenis (ITP), and research what the Bible says about healing. He sought strong minded Christians in his field but was disappointed to find that most of other clergyman doesn't know about this condition, but they does believe in the power of prayer to healing.

So author write about his experience with the condition and share it with other whom experience the same thing. He will travel the world and take some unusual path in his quest for supernatural healing through Jesus Christ. Surely there were those who still believed in God and Jesus Christ power to healing through prayer.

Most likely this sickness was addressed primarily through prayer for healing power. Author tells us at the outset what the experience in intended to teach; men and women ought always to pray, and not to faint. More than one observer has remarked that God has three answers for our prayers. One is Yes, another is No, and a third is Wait a while. Most of us have been perplexed by a firm No in answer to a fervent prayer. Wait a while is not much less perplexing. Not until the while of waiting is over can we distinguish it from a No.

Do you ever feel like, after the prayer, there is no response? Are you impatient for an answer, like some people. Why are God's answers often so long in coming? We pray for loved one who is suffering from some illness. We pray for healing, or we pray for release from pain, and yet our loved one finds neither healing nor release for weeks, or months, or years. sometimes it may be for the witness the suffering one has. When pain is endured patiently, it is a testimony to the sustaining power of faith and of Jesus Christ, who is the "author and finisher of our faith" Hebrews 12:2.

It testifies to medical staff and visitors, to the saints and to the lost. In Hezekiah case it even testified of healing power through prayer. Sometimes it may be for the growth of the sufferer. James wrote, "My brethren, count it all joy" James 1:2-4.

In the meantime, we may wonder if our faith is deficient, for Lord Jesus Christ promised to grant the prayer of a believer in Mark 11:24. Some pray selfish prayer and tried to disguise it by saying, "In Jesus name." But the Jesus Christ is not fooled. He knows when a prayer is really in our own name. And most of us must admit that at times we do not know what to pray for. We can only trust the Holy Spirit to carry the proper request to the Father with an urgency beyond words in Romans 8: 26-217.

The author is brings us his experience with as death disease, and three example on prayer, and in these there is not much perplexity. In each case, author lets us know clearly what the experience is designed to teach. Let us learn that man of God can help. In the case of Hezekiah he look for salvation at such a critical hour? See now what Hezekiah did. He tells us all what to do in any time of trouble. The first thing that Hezekiah did was to go straight into the house of the Lord means "church". He took his burden into the sanctuary. And that is what the house of the Lord is for.

It is a place of refuge for the harassed soul of man or woman beset with danger from which he or she sees no escape. How many since the day of Hezekiah have done the same thing, and have found deliverance there.

When he tried to understand it, he became perplexed and bewildered; until he went into the sanctuary of God. Then his burden was lifted; then he came to understand what it all meant; then his vision became clear; then his knowledge of God's encompassing love became strong. There he found rest for his soul, and out of this experience he wrote the history which begins and ends in the note of faith and thanksgiving.

So it is with men and women today. So long as all goes well with them they may pass by the sanctuary and give it no place in their lives. But let sorrow come, or danger, let life prove too much for them and failure bring pride to the ground, then they flee for refuge, just as Hezekiah did, to the house of the Lord. It stands there always, ready to receive them. The church is "the mother of us all" Gal. 4:26. It is ready to receive its children in every time of need.

The power of prayer of Hezekiah, then, through his emissaries told Isaiah how affairs stool. Was it possible that the God of Isaiah, the Lord God, would hear the taunts of the Assyrians and answer them? Human wisdom did not know how to say? Wherefore life up thy prayer. Here is expressed faith in the intercessory prayer of one whose heart was right toward God. However skeptical one may be about the efficacy of one's own prayers, there remains nethermost in the hearts of most men and women an inarticulate, unreasoned, but inextinguishable faith in the prayers of man of God.

Hezekiah is a good example that prayer can change thing. The human diagnosis was correct. But this omitted the possibility of a spiritual cure; the immediate contact of the soul with God, the immediate impact of the life of God on soul and body. That prayer is a powerful agency in the healing of the sick is now generally admitted by medical science. The author have seen men, women, and children after all other therapy had failed, lifted out of disease . . . by the serene effort of prayer.

It is the only power in the world that seems to overcome the so-called laws of nature. But note that Isaiah did not neglect materia medica. He applied first aid and laid figs on the diseased spot. A sick man oe woman needs two things which should always go together; prayer and the doctor. Neither should exclude the other. They combine and cooperate in the healing of the sick. Yet Isaiah was careful to remind the Hezekiah that it was not the figs but the Lord God who healing him in answer to his prayer. In II Kings 20:5. Two answered prayers in Hezekiah's life. Could he ever forget that?

When Hezekiah wanted proof that he was to recover, Isaiah suggested a miraculous setting back of the shadow on the sundial of Ahaz. Thus by outward sign was confirmed the turning back of the disease of the Hezekiah. Whatever we think of this extraordinary incident, it points to a profound and often forgotten truth that God is not bound by what we call the laws of nature.

He is a free moral agent at the heart of the universe, a self-governing and self-determining personality possessing freedom and initiative, not controlled by the universe but in a real sense controlling and operating it; not limited by its laws except in so far as he chooses to be limited by them; not allowing perpetual variation on the suggestion of occasional moral contingencies, yet always governing according to the principles of his being. In Hezekiah case prayer does change things. Two prayers answered, and yet forgetting God!

Sometimes the life of good man or good women ends in moral anti-climax. No man or woman's life can be finally assessed until the very last day of it has been lived. Hezekiah and other people who have longtime illness had a chance to be spiritual healing. The story of the man who was sick, named Lazarus, of Bethany, the town of Mary and her sister Martha. Jesus Christ says: "This sickness is not unto death, but for the glory of God, that the Son of God might be glorified thereby". John 11:1.

You know the story that Lazarus death. Sometime things does not go like we thing if should go or happened because we does not have faith in God and His Son Jesus Christ. Jesus says to the two sister "And I am glad for your sakes that I was not there, to the intent ye may believe; nevertheless let us go unto him." John 11:15. Many people have some kind of sickness or illness that needed spiritual healing. Because of the sin infect the blood to cause disease in by allowing germs or bacteria to enter the blood.

The author point out from Old and New Testament used the designative of the blood, the red fluid that flows in the veins of men, women, children, and animals. In recent times the idea has grown up that blood is also used to denote life released from the flesh. Some Old Testament passages held to indicate that the Hebrews thought of life as somehow resident in the blood, so that, when an animal's blood was shed for the life of the flesh is in the blood: and I have given it to upon the altar to make atonement for your soul: for it is the blood that maketh atonement by reason of the life. Issaiah 49:26; Matt. 26:28. In accord with widespread belief, blood when shed had uncanny power; it called down vengeance was assured by God. It had a central role in ritual; in sacrifices it was set apart and applied to sacred objects, symbols of the divine presence and power. Being so near, the divine, blood is holy and efficacious. It moves sin and consecrates. According to the New Testament, the blood of Christ offered in the Pasion achieves once and for all the whole aim of rites prescribed by the Law, Purity and Unity.

According to Romans 3:24-25 expiation has been made by the blood so that redemption from sin has finally been effects. The blood is Jesus, because the blood of Christ cleanses the conscience from dead works for the service of the living God. The major ideas in this book focus on the Good and Evil that contain in this book. The authors focus on awareness of how we perceive others and ourselves. This cultural conditioning limits our ability to benefit from what has been created by God.

Today we have increasing opportunities to enrich ourselves because we truly the Lord Jesus Christ, in person or through media, to cultures different from our own. But the value of such experience depends on our respect for and appreciation of the Lord thou God. If we fail to keep an open mind, we will succeed only in Jesus Christ. Our method is to offer you a series of concepts, based on our previous experience with the subject, and a certain amount of preliminary knowledge.

As you see evidence to support these concepts, you'll select and reject so, and an amount will remain with you. But it will be even more gratifying when you start asking new questions and additional concepts of your own. Eventually, you may find, as we have, that answers to small questions about Diseases, in our societies, Christianity and philosophies begin to add up to some big conclusion about mankind's behavior.

Of course, you will want to test these conclusion further, which means you will have to ask some more questions and you will need more medical information. So the process begins again, but now at a higher yet deeper level. Since you already knows quite a lot. At this point, you will probably not only start reviewing the medical materials you already have but begin looking for addition material in medical book, magazines, internet, and other information. The authors focus his attention on the story from the Bible dealt with healing; a woman who have a issue of blood.

The condition here translated be made well; carries with it idea of rescue from impeccant destruction or from a superior power. This story is like the Shunammite woman about her son. The woman with the issue of blood contains two lesson of importance to us. In the first place we are reminded of the Sex and Spiritual healing. Matt. 9:20 reads, "And, behold, a woman, which was diseased with an issue of blood twelve years, came behind him, and touch the hem of his garment." The precise nature of the woman's sickness is not understood. This chapter is concerned with secretions connected with the sexual organs. We may concur Matthew wrote, "For she said within herself, If I may but touch his garment, I shall be whole", we may note, too, with Matthew and Jesus Christ that a sense of natural disgust or shame has been developed into an sex and spiritual healing feeling of cleanness.

But, in fact, there is an almost necessary connection between sex and spiritual healing because both belong to the spher of the sacred. There have been those who have sought to live as if the sexual had no place in their lives. This leads to disaster. Not less disastrous is a purely materialistic or Sinful Diseases purely physical notion of sex.

Woman is neither an angel nor a beast, but a person compact of body and soul in indissoluble union while life lasts. The consulting rooms of the psychoanalysts are thronged with people who have failed to see the connection between sex and spiritual healing. The ancient rules of this chapter have no direct relecance for us. A guiding principle for Christians is that the sexual nature of woman or man must be frankly recognized by him or her and accepted, and must also be kept in its due place by reverence for his or her spiritual nature.

It would seem that she said within herself, if I but touch his mean "Jesus" garment, she shall be whole. If this is true, the present passage may represent faith in his garment. This statement appears to be addressed to Jesus Christ. Probably some sort of sex disease caused the bleeding that had pressed for twelve years. She had suffered much, had been treated by many physicians, had spent all she had; instead of getting better, her condition had gotten worse. She heard about Jesus Christ healings, she can be healing of her condition. She believe with faith, that Jesus can healed her; if I just touch, the bleeding will stopped, and she felt a soundness in her body that assured her that she had been healed.

But Jesus turned him about, and when he saw her, he said, "Daughter, be of good comfort; thy faith hath made thee whole." The phrase "comfort" freedom from pain. And the woman was made whole from that hour. The problem of healing is no longer a question of attaining a moral ideal, but a stark necessity for the continued existence of man, or woman. It is clear that is woman has the capacity to solve every problem except the problem of self-control.

That victory awaits her, and must continue to avoid her until she acknowledged the need of power other than her own to change her life. Jesus Christ saw it long age, and this is the message of his prophecy of reconciliation. Spiritual healing is not basically a matter of treaties but of a new spiritual healing in human relationship, and that new spiritual healing is possible only through a shared faith, trust, and obedience to God. It is so easy to write this or say it, but little short of an agony to bring men and women to accept it as God's condition for spiritual healing on earth. The alternative is before us, a godless civilization moving to its own doom and damnation, or a race which has found its salvation and its peace in a common faith and obedience to Almighty God. Is there yet to be a day when the oracle shall reads, "Blessed be American, my people, and the whole world, the work of my hands, And the Commonwealth of Nations, my inheritance?"

The woman was free of pain. The story of the woman made clear to the author that it was her faith in Jesus Christ; called a change in her life. Here both sex and spiritual healing involve; the two are closely together. The words of Jesus to the woman, be freed from your suffering he actively participated in her healing and confirmed God's will to make her well. Pray can chang thing.

CHAPTER 4

Seven Deadly Sins

At an early stage in the church, the influence of Greek thought, with its tendency to view sin as a necessary flow in human nature; made it necessary for the church to determine the relative seriousness of various moral faults. This ultimately gave rise to what is commonly referred to as the seven deadly sins; a concept which occupies an important place in the order and discipline of the Roman Catholic Church, and other Churches too. These sins are: Pride, Covetousness, Lust, Envy, Gluttony angers, and Sloth.

Pride may be defined as inordinate and unreasonable self-esteem, attended with insolence and rule treatment of others. Pride is universal among all notions, being variously attributed in the Bible. It is connected with the sin of Sodom. Indeed, the ambitious pride of Satan was part of the original sin of the universe. It was well have been the first sin to enter God's universe, and no doubt will be one of the last to be conquered. The Bible teaches that pride deceives the heart, hardens the mind, brings contention, compasses about like a chain, and brings men to destruction. A proud heart stirs up strife, and is an abomination into the Lord. A proud look God hates, and those who engage therein shall stumble and fall. Pride is the parent of discontent, ingratitude, presumption, passion, extravagance, and bigotry.

There is hardly an evil committed without pride being connected in some sense. Some Christian held that pride was the very essence of sin. Since Jesus Christ resists the proud, the believer must learn to dislike pride and to clothe himself or herself with humility being humble. The Bible teaches that pride deceives the heart in Jeremiah 49:16, you will learn that God's says; "Though thou shouldest make thy nest as high as the eagle, I will bring thee down from thence, saith the Lord." Hardens the mind in Daniel 5:20, in brings contention in Proverbs 13: 10, compass about like a chain in Psalms 73:6 pride cause violence.

Pride is their necklace; ill-temper, violence covers them as a garment gluttony: their eyes swell out with fatness; wanton folly, their hearts overflow with follies; humorless malice; boastfulness, loftily they threaten oppression; and arrogant impiety, they set their mouths against the heavens, and their tongue struts through the earth. Pride will bring men and women to destruction in Proverbs 16:18 also spoken of pride is considered a Christians offense against God.

1.   Pride prevents growth. When a man or woman is sure that he or she knows everything there is to be known he or she is not in a frame of mind to learn anything from others. A man or woman who is blind to his or her own defects has little chance to correct themselves. The sages have little good to say about a fool, but they think that there is more hope for a fool than for a man or woman wise in his or her own conceit. A proud look God hates in Proverbs 6:17 reads, "A proud look, a lying tongue, and hands that shed innocent blood." We should note the part of the human body mentioned in the verse 17.

The God who is described in this chapter is no indifferent God who has no preferences. There are some things of which God disapproves. He hates them. The author is writer from the Holy Bible regarding Seven Deadly Sin; the writer is indeed courageous in assuming that the Scripture knows what God hates. The probability is that author picked out some human attitudes that were hateful to him and proved damaging in humanb relations, and then asserted that God also disapproves of them.

He could not believe that something could be good in God's sight if it was evil in his human sight. Though years have passed since King Solomon made this judgment, few would assert that a faithful Creator would not still disapprove of such attitudes as he describes. Five of the seven things hateful to God are pictured in terms of parts of the human body: named "Eyes, Tongue, Hands, Heart, and Feet. Note, none of these organs is hateful in itself; the divine disapproval arises when the man or woman uses his or her eyes to flaunt his or her haughtiness, his or her tongue to lie, his or her hands to shed innocent blood, his or her heart and mind to devise crafty plans, and his or her feet to run some evil errand.

The word of Jesus Christ come to mind, "Wherefore if thy hand or thy foot offend thee, cut them off, and cast them from thee: it is better for thee to enter into life halt or maimed, rather than having two hands or two feet to be cast into everlasting fire" Matt.18:8. It should be notice that this chapter is left by itself, it presents a God with a strong words to His preacher. God is more interested in making plain what He hates than He is intent upon indicating what He loves. And yet all love implies rejection of that which harms the loved one. All love of beauty implies a rejection of the ugly. A God who hates nothing could hardly be said to love anything, but we have a God who has the nature to hate and to disapprove the attitudes that frustrate his good purposes for men and women. The man or woman who seaches for the divine approval, who longs to hear the "Well done, good and faithful servant" Matt.25:21, will avoid those things which must be disapproved by God of all mankind.

2. Covetousness means primaril inordinate desire. It has come to mean a desire for anything which is inordinate in degree, or a desire for that which rightfully belongs to another, especially in the realm of material things. In a general sense it means all inordinate desire for wordly possessions, such as honors or gold. In a more restricted sense, it's a desire for the increasing of one's substance by appropriating that of others.

The shades of meaning vary according to the particular word used and the context. Covetousness is a grave sin. It is labeled idolatry in Colossians 3:5, for intensity of desire and worship are closely related. Its heinousness doubtless is accounted for by its being, in a very real sense, the root of many forms of sin. This is the reason Jesus Christ warned against it so sternly in Luke 12:15. It should be notice that some say preachers should not meddle with such matters; but did not our Savior Jesuse Christ meddle with matters of judgment, when he spake of the wicked judge, to leave example to us to follow, to do the same?

The Holy Scripture qualifieth the officers, and sheweth what manner of men they should be, and of what qualities them. First, men of activity, that have stomachs meant: courage" to do their duty; they must not be milksops mean "unmanly man", nor white-livered knights mean "takeover viewed as unfavorable"; they must be wise, hearty, hardy, men of a good stomach.

Secondarily, he qualifieth them with the fear of God, for if he fear God, he shall be no briber, no perverted of judgment, faithful. Thirdly, they must be chosen men, in whom is truth, if God's say it, it shall be done. Fourthly, hating covetousness; far from it, he will not come near it that hateth it; such as be meet to be office, seek them out, hire them, give them competent and liberal fees, that they shall not need to take any bribes. It should be notice that an sermon preached before King Edward VI. This was plain speaking before the king, and preachers who would emulate him should remember that Latimer a "Protestant Bishop and religious reformer" who was burned at the stake six years afterward.

3.   Lust is a desire to gratify the senses; bodily appetite, sexual desire as seeking unrestrained gratification. The question of desire was much discussed in Greek ethics; but didn't command a dominant interest in the New Testament. Numerous words are used to express the same general idea. They possess no necessary moral connotation, but because of the sinful nature of man they came generally to describe wrong desire. Concuoiscence is the equivalent of the Greek usually translated "lust" but occasionally, concupiscence and in a good sense. It signifies for the most part the wrongful inclination of the sinner which characterizes his or her nature and leads to sinful acts.

While allowing that it's sinful in the unregenerate, medieval and Romanist theologians argue that it is only the testing scar and combustible material of sin in the baptized, in whom original sin is supposed to the abolished. But reformation theology does not accept this distinction or its presupposition. Although not imputed, original sin remains in believers, and therefore concupiscence may and must be said to have of it's the, true and proper, nature of sin.

If a man or woman lust upon a man or woman's he or she desired that person. In the "desire" more often "lust" in eight passages. It should be notice that "lust" is the greatly sin to man. This include day rape, and intercourse with a forcibly, and without her or his consent. It also cover under Deuteronomic Code, the man is order to compensate of the action or offender.

King David desire a man wife. He was as king was an high court judge. It was therefore natural that he should be consulted about a difficult point of law. King David has Uriah kill in battle to take his wife. The history tells us, everything had been made right except David's relationship to God. Therefore everything done both that which brought forth sin, and that which sought to rectify the situations created out of sin was wrong.

The worst thing about war, for instance, is the complete lack of humility and repentance with which we declare our participation in a "righteous" endeavor which is in reality our sinful attempt to avoid the consequences of previous selfish living. It should be notice that David's attempts at rectification came as completely under the heading "displeasing to God" as did his original sin. The penalties of sin in high. If you reads, II Samuel 12: 13-23, you will understand sin against God from the sin of king David.

There is a sense in which all human sin is in high places. God made man "a little lower than the angels, and crowned him with glory and honor" Psalms 8:5. He is infinitely above the animal, and when he sins, he inevitably violates the image of God within himself. "Be yourself" is a high and holy one. "Know ye not that ye are the temple of God, and that the Spirit of God dwelleth in you?" I Cor.3:16.

To be a man, not just an animal, is a high calling; to forswear manhood in favor of the satisfaction of animal instincts is to reverse the whole purpose of God for man and woman. This is sin with a capital "S". The punishment is severe because the sin is great. A most helpful analysis of this great text is presented from the viewpoint of a King David and others men and women today.

Let me explain "Sin against God". Herein is revealed the spiritual stature of David. He repents his having exercised the prerogatives of pagan kings; he recognizes the true nature of sin, rebellion against God. his sin represented a threefold assault against God's sovereignty. (1) As a man of God, he was disobedient. (2) As an especially chosen and dedicated representative of God, he dishonored the King whose ambassador he was. (3) As a ruthless disrupter of fine human relationships, he sinned against other man of God, and so against the whole covenant purpose of God.

It should be notice that man's sin, Jesus coming, and God's forgiveness save mankind. When a seminary of theological professor was asked which he believed to be the greatest of the psalms, he replied without hesitation, "King David's." When asked to be more explicit, he named II Samuel 12:1-24; Psalms 32:1-2; 51:1 130; and 143. These, it is hardly necessary to say, are four of the penitential psalms. There will be some, perhaps many, who will immediately add that the verdict shows how far the great reformer is removed from the modern world. We know the modern world, is not worrying itself about sin.

There we must at once join issue. The modern world does not accept the words of seminary of theological professor, but there is nothing the world is more worried about than "sin"; the thing, if not the word. It may be someone else's lust or sin, which only shows how low we have fallen; but human sin is the ultimate problem, the one subject that is always worth discussing. St. Paul says, "All have sinned, and come short of the glory of God." Romans 3:23. Luke 20:46; 15:16; 10:24, but because of the sinful nature of man they came generally to describe wrong desire. In Matt. 5:28 is used specifically of sexual desire, understood as contravention of the law. In the New Testament Epistles the noun has become fixed as a description of lust.

4.   Envy is always means bad, jealousy, and zeal are frequently good. similarly to eye and the evil eyed. Jealousy is used is the Scripture of the emotion inspired by the infringing or denial of the right of exclusive possession. It describes the attitude of God toward the infringement of the right to the exclusive worship and service of his people. God is jealous God; his name is jealous, and he is very leadous for his Holy name; and also for the good name and well-being of his people and of his holy city.

This appears in the Old Testament, as an attribute to God, in the sense of his desiring to maintain a unique and pure relation between himself and Israel. The word jealous is related etymologically to zealous, which renders the same Hebrew and Greek words. I Sam. 18:9; Ecclesiastes 14: 8-10; Matt. 20:1`5; and Mark 7:22. But envy to Joseph's brethren, Saul towards David and the chief priests toward Jesusd Christ has reference to an inalienable possession, paternal love, victorious honors of spiritual greatness; while jealousy and zeal, good and bad in Gal. 4:17-18, relate to alterable circumstances. Envy is essentially devilish in I John 3:12; and a work of the flesh in Gal. 5:21, and was a "deadly sin" in later moral theology.

5.   Glutton is a man or woman who greedily eats to much; a person with a great capacity for something. God's said, "If a man have a stubborn and rebellious son, which will not obey the voice of his father, or the voice of his mother, and that, when they've chastend him, will not hearken unto them." Since the stability of the family is basic to stable community life, respect for and obedience to the parents were of vital importance to the Israelite community with the Fifth Commandment.

In the Book of the Covenant a son who smites or curses his parents shall receive the death penalty in Exodus 21:15-17; Lev. 20:9, and in the old list of curses quoted in Deut 27, the son who "setteth light by his father or her mother" is accursed in verse 16. In the Scripture before us the completely hardened and worthless son is to be done away. This is not to be done by the parents themselves, but by the community after a judicial decision by the elders.

In this manner the community purges itself of the festering sore of evil. The father of the son did not have the power of life and death over his son; his complaint must be decided before an impartial court. It is highly improbable that parents often appealed to such a law as this. In Deuteronomy, unlike its predecessors, the cause may be protracted disobedience as well as cursing or smiting a parent.

In thus placing the power of life and death in the community, this law is somewhat better than was the case with the Roman father who himself had the power of life and death over his child. Judaism and Christianity have long since ceased to condone such practices, though of course we do not condemn the occasional parent who may before to seek civil help in restraining willful children. Proverbs 23:21; Matt. 11:19; Luke 7:34.

6. Anger is generally means Wrath and Indignation are integral to the biblical proclamation of the living God in his opposition to sin. While God's love is spontaneous to his own being; his wrath is called forth by the wickedness of his people. Wrath is the effect of human sin, mercy is not the effect of human goodness, but is inherent in the character of God.

In the Old Testament wrath is the expression of the personal, subjecttive free will of Christian who actively punishes sin, as in the New Testament, it's the personal reaction of God; not an independent hypostasis. In the face of evil, the Holy One of Israel doesn't dodge the responsibility of executing judgment. He demonstrate his anger at times in the most personal way possible. The wrath of God is being continually revealed from heaven, actively giving the wicked up to uncleanness, to passions, to reprobate minds, and punishing them in the day of wrath and revelation of the just judgment. Throughout the Bible, the wrath of God is not much an emotion or an angry frame of mind as it's the settled opposition of his holiness to evil. Accordingly, the wrath of God is seen in its effects, in God's punishment of sin in this life and in the future. In the New Testamant the call is to faith, to repentance, to baptism in the name of the Lord Jesus Christ who saves us from the wrath to come in I Thessalonians 1:9-10. For when we are justified by his blood and reconciled by his death we shall be saved from the wrath by his life in Romans 5:9-10. The most poignan word about God's punishment is that it is the wrath of the Lamb, who took upon himself and bore the sins of the world.

7. Sloth is the general terms refer to extremely dull, unresponsive or inactive states due to laziness, sluggish health, or mental depression. Classically one of the seven deadly sins, sloth stresses extreme inaction due to laziness, a state amenable to a simple effort of the will. The word is sharp its disapproval and suggest the unpleasant concomitants of sloppiness, untidiness, or unseemliness; filthy, disheveled rooms that gove eloquent testimony to his or her life of sloth and debauchery.

    Sloth at its most general can indicate as they apply to people who do not accomplish things quickly or to actions which consume a great deal of time, often more than is thought necessary. Slow is the general term means extending or occurring over a relatively long span of time. Slow may be positive in its application to persons; a slow but meticulous craftsman, a person slow to anger. It may also suggest such undesirable traits as laziness or stupidity; slow in a person work because they talk constantly to follow workers; a person of such limited ability that he or she is slow to understand the simplest directions. Ecclessiastes 10:18; Proverbs 12:24-27; and Matt. 25:26.

CHAPTER 5

The Sheep and The Goats

The language of this book reminds us of the parable of our Lord Jesus Christ regarding the Sheep and the Goats, as the image employed is that of a shepherd sorting out his sheep by means of his rod. But here those who are as it were on the left hand are not sent away into everlasting punishment. They are actually brought out of the country where they sojourn and in so far delivered. But they do not enter into the kingdom of God, they remain outside the final blessing of their people.

Why is that? Not because of a divine sentence of judgment perhaps, but simply because tthere would be, as we say, no place for them there. The mere circimstance that our suffering has been ended will not bring us to new life unless we are spiritually prepared for it. And if in our suffering we have been rebellious we shall not be thus prepared. We need to revival himself or herself. The first condition of such a revival is decision. The state of affairs in which God is only one of several allegiances must be ended.

Men and women decide for him or her against him or her in verse 39. This does not mean that we have the freedom to ignore the needs of any who are not followers of Jesus Christ did not do this during His earthly ministry, and neither should His people. As we have therefore opportunity, let us do good unto all men, and women, especially unto them who are Christian.

St. Matthew 25:31-33 telling, when Jesus Christ comes, He will send His angels to gather His people from all parts of the earth in St. Matt. 24:-30-31. Those follower of Jesus Christ who have died will be restored to life and gathered along with those who have not died in I Thessalonians 4:16-17. This book reminds us that the people who do not belong to Jesus Christ will be gathered as well, whether they have died or not, gathered for the great Judgment Day in on 5:28-29. This is an oppointment that all must keep in Hebrews 9:27, and Matt. 25:32.

If you notice verse 32, all the people of all nations and all times will be gathered before Jesus Christ on this day. Can you imagine the countless trillions of people or billion of peoples? Tey the judge will evaluate each one individually, separating them one from another, and it will not be difficult for Him to do. A shepherd does not need a series of tests to tell a sheep from a goat; a mere glance is enough. In the same way, the all knowing judge recognizes instantly whether a person is His or not. The identity of an individual is apparent in what he or she has done or failed to do.

We need to understand that there are two biblical principles that must be kept in balance. One is that of remaining separate from the world in I Corinthians 15:33; II Corinthians 6:14-18; Hebrews 7:26; James 1:27; I John 2:15. The other is that of having an influence for good on the people of the world in Matt. 5:13-16; I Corinthians 7:16; Philippians 2:15. Jesus Christ was criticized for associating with "sinners", but He continued to associate with them in order to bring them to repentance.

Discuss how much a Christian can associate with unbelievers before compromising his or her witness. What are some things a believer should never do in associating, even for a good cause, with unbelievers? What are Some things a believer might do, even if other Christians were uncomfortable with it, in order to reach out to the lost? I am begin to think and writer like a philosophy. I am a "Philosophy".

If you notice verse 33, throughout history the right hand for a ruler has been considered a place of honor. Jesu Christ own people will be placed there in recognition of what their actions have shown them to be. Do you know, the Berlin wall stood for twenty eight years as a concrete symbol of the cold war, concrete in more ways than one.

First, it was made of steel reinforced slabs of concrete that sliced through the heart of Berlin, Germany. It was also concrete, not abstract, as a tengible and visible symbol of the philosophical chasm that separated the free world from the communist bloc of nations.

The west offered freedom and increasing prosperity. The East's only appeal was the drabness of a collective society where the possibility for economic success was as limited as the opportunity for political self-determination. The difference between the two sectors created a kind of "sheep and goats" scenario; on the one side, the blessings of a free society; on the other, the confining restrictions of a repressive system.

When the crumbling foundations of communism finally caused the Berlin Wall to fall on November 9, 1989., Germans on both sides of the border rejoiced at the reunification now made possible, and the world rejoiced with them. While the strict separation represented by the Berlin Wall eventually ceased, the "sheep and goats" separation on Judgment Day will be enternally permanent. And it will be based, not on the caprice of political fortune, but on the decision each of us has made as to which side we have given allegiance.

It should be notice that Jesus Christ, the failure Judge, has examined the people from all nations, and the has separated the sheep from the goats. He was addresses the sheep, who have been placed at His right hand in verse 34. To inherit the kingdom is not merely to have a place in it, it is to inherit the kingship or to be a king.

Thus, amid the magnificent visions of Revelation, the apostle John heard these words of praise addressed to Jesus Christ the Lamb, in Rev. 5:9-10. If we stand with the redeemed of Jesus Crist hand, shall we be equal to Jesus Christ himself? No, we shall be kings, but He will be king of kings in Rev. 17:14. "His servants shall serve him". Rev. 22:3, but they shall reign for ever and ever in Rev. 22:5.

If we rule with Jesus Christ forever, who will be our subjects? Whom shall we rule? Shall we not rule ourselves and each other? Every king will be a subject, and every subject will be a king; for no one will be ruled against his will. Can you imagine yourself so well attuned to everything true and right that every desire of your heart will also be a desire of God's heart?

What Heavenly harmony! That kingdom eternal, that land of perfect harmony, will be neither an accident nor an after thought in the mind of God. From the foundation of the world it has been prepared for those who will align themselves with God's Son in I Peter 1:18-20.

We should notice that the reason in verse 35-36, on His royal throne the judge describes, one by one, some of the most common needs and distresses of mankind; hunger, thirst, loneliness in a stronge place, lack of clothing, illness, and imprisonment. The Judge has experienced all of these situations, he says, and those people who are now his right hand have helped him bear the burden of them. That is the reason they are receiving the blessing described in verse 34.

Will the righteous ask the question in verser 37-39. Remember who these righteous are; they are followers of Jesus Christ who have been gathered from all nations of the world in verse 32, and throughout all centuries of history. Very few of them have seen Jesus Christ before, here they view him enthroned in glory. When did they ever have the opportunity to help him in a time of need or distress?

Jesus Christ give us an explanation in verse 40. Most of the righteous people in verse 37 have not seen Jesus Christ in person before His appearance on the judgment throne, but they have seen others in need. They have seen some of the righteous in distress and have helped them. Jesus Christ calls these righteous people my brethren. We are calls brethren because of Jesus Christ. But to those who believe in Him, He gives the right to become sons of God in a different way; for in a different way they too are born of God in John 1:12-13, Therefore "he is not ashamed to call them brethren" in Hebrews 2:11.

And all the help given to those "brethren" He counts as help given to Him personally. This does not mean that we have the freedom to ignore the needs of any who are not followers of Jesus Christ. Jesus Christ did not do this during His earthly ministry, and neither should His people.

Paul's words in Galatians 6:10 are instructive on this matter. As we have therefore opportunity, let us do good unto all men, and momen, especially unto them who are of the household of faith. We have learn about the "Sheep" on the right hand. Jesus Christ turns to the "Goats" on the left. In light of Jesus Christ words recorded in Matt. 7:13-14, you should notice that the throng on the left is much larger that the one on the right.

Matthew 25:41-45 speak of the "goats" are cursed. All the people of all nations and all times will be gathered before Jesus Christ on that Great Day. The Evil One who is "Satan" and his angels (demons) will be gathered before Jesus Christ. Matt. 25:41 raeds, "Then shall he say also unto them on the left hand, Depart from me, ye cursed, into everlasting fire, prepared for the devil and his angels".

It should be notice that one group is invited to come, the other is ordered to depart. One is called blessed; the other is called cursed. One is called to a kingdom, the other is sent to everlasting fire. Those who are sheep inherit a kingdom prepared for them. Those who are goats have no place prepared for them; they can only share the place prepared for the Satan and his angels.

There is nowhere else to go. It should be notice that Hell is not a place prepared for the righteousness, or other to be. God wants no one to go there reads II Peter 3:9. Notice how observe that these people condemned to everlasting fire are not accused of doing anthing maliciously evil; no murder, mayhem, assault, adultery, arson, or theft. They are condemned for doing nothing. They had opportunities to do good, just as the the people on the right; but they chose to do nothing.

One thing we can do is to be sure a portion of out church budget is designated for benevolence offering. That way, every time we put money into the offering basket, we are doing something to help the needy. Of course, we need to look for personal opportunities to help as well. It is easy to get busy doing "good thing" not "bad thing" but the better thing is to reach out and help those who are in need.

Verse 44, speaking most of these on Jesus left had never seen Him. In this, they were like those on the right. Seeing Him now upon the trone of his glory in verse 31, they could hardly believe that He had ever been a victim of poverty or imprisinment. Were they being condemned unjustly? Notice that verse 45, the great majority of those at Jesus Christ left hand have not seen Him before that Judgment Day, but they have seen many of His people, those who have been born again as children of God, whom Jesus calls His brethren. They have seen some of those brethren in need and have neglected to help them. Jesus Christ takes that neglect personally, as if He Himself were neglected. For that neglect, the people on the left are sent from the presence of Jesus Christ into everlasting fire.

The author notes that we do not have the freedom to ignore the needs of any who are not followers of Jesus Christ in Galatians 6:10. "As we have therefore opportunity, let us do good unto all men, especially unto them who are of the houshold of faith." We have a program in place to be sure we care for those who are members of our church. We need to help other congregation, and faith.

This will help the members and testify to the community of our love for the "Church program." But each person believer ought to be quick to render aid to a neighbor or anyone else in need, regardless of whether the person is a member of the church or not. This too will be a testimony to the community and will help to win the lost.

It should be notice that verse 46 states "And these shall go away into everlasting punishment: but the righteous into life eternal." The people placed at Jesus Christ right hand in the final judgment really will inherit the kingdom prepared for them from the foundation of the world. Those placed at His left really will be banished to everlasting fire prepared for the Satan and his angels.

So each one of us struggles with his or her own decisions. Which of the needy shall I help, and how much shall I help them? Each person makes his or her own choice, and no two choices are alike. But let each person remember that he or she is choosing more than where he or she will spend his or her money.

There is yet more to the rest of the story. Jesus is prophecy of the final judgment where everyone in the world can see God the Father, and the Son Jesus Christ. When people stop to think about the final judgment, they become filled with a variety of reactions. What words, thoughts, or emotions come into your mind when you think of "Final Judgment"?

Some people look on the final judgment favorably, while others express fear and dread. Today's people does not think about the final judgment. They think about living today and tomorring. The author is showing in this book "Good and Evil" from Matthews 25:31-46 presents the separation that will occur in the final judgment and encourages us to prepare for Jesus Christ return.

Before we continue others event happen before the final judgment to make certain that we understand what the text tells about Jesus Christ prophecy of the final judgment, let's briefly retell the some facts before the final judgment.

The Old Testament abounds with portrayals of character in which the spiritual problem is always central and in which hero is conceived in terms of faith and obedience. The author is remind, as for example between Abram and Lot, Moses and the people, Samuel and Saul, Elihah and Ahab, Isaiah and Ahaz, Jeremiah and Zedekiah. The first name in each case is that of a man who possessed a wholeness and soundness of character.

The close relationship existing between him and God was unimpaired by irresolution in faith and obedience. It is not that he was sinless, "Abram and Moses", but that he possessed a wholesome relationship to God, with the result that through him God's work was done. This is what the Hebrew people called "tamim", inadequately rendered as "perfect" in English.

The second parties in the above pairs are not "perfect"; a barrier exists between them and God. Therefore they are not spiritually whole, they are weak, and their weakness issues in over acts of sin. It should be known that, it is this aspect of the conception of sin in the Bible which so differentiates it from the conceptions of wrongdoing in other beliefs.

Sin as the personal violation of one's relationship with God, as the involvement of one's whole being in a haughty and rebellious act, and as the destruction of one's normal, healthy, and dependent integrity such an analysis of the meaning of man and woman's evil is completely unknown elsewhere.

In the Bible there many words denoting evil acts, but none of them are properly rendered "sin" in the biblical sense. The above statements about the sin or lack of it, in human life seem capable of being applied to other religions, ancient and modern. In no biblical faith does there occur such a radical, profound, and penetrating view of human error as that occasioned by the doctrine of God in the Bible.

The Satan understood man or woman as subject to the divine will and decree, but he knew nothing of the righteousness of God in the biblical sense and the question of sin did not enter their minds. The problem of man or woman in worship was to isolate and identify the particular offense which had angered the gods and to make the specific penance prescribed for its expiation. Human error was thus atomized and its remedy mechanistic.

In any event, such sinners could appeal only in repentance to God directly; their sacrifice could not make atonement for man or woman. where there are gross sins, the occasion for which is a hard or uncircumcised, heart, a stiff neck, a "spirit of whoredom" that is, where man or woman is clearly rebelling against the covenant presence of God, then the sacrificial law which was given to the Christian community was no longer efficacious. It should be notice that the laws for worship were given to the "church", the Christian community of the faithful. If one cut himself or herself off from the "church" by flagrant sins, either of an interior or evert nature, or both, then he or she must not expect the law to cover his or her situation.

Does the gross sinner, then, have no hope? People's knowledge of the gracious nature of God was so deep that he or she possessed an extraording of his or her forgiveness. Before the holiness and covenant presence of God the gross sinner stands condemned.

God's forgiveness means that he or she desires to repair the communion and to restore the offender into the sacred fellowship with himself or herself and his or her fellows in the congregation of the church. As you known that other religions of today are knew of divine holiness and goodness, as also of divine grace to those whom the gods deemed worthy of it.

But this biblical forgiving, love, the purpose of which was to create Christian community and to repair the breach between it and God, is as phenomenal as it is unique. It is radically different from the subtle, modern idolatry in the church which assumes that of course God will forgive because it is his primary business to do so.

When God does these things, the person will possess a "clean heart" and a "right spirit". Psalm 51:10. The difficulty of the sinner is that he or she is "cast away" from God's presence and removed from the working of his or her spirit; but in forgiveness there is restoration unto "the joy of the salvation" in Psalm 51:11-12.

A very common expression for forgiveness is "to take away" or "to carry away" sin, Jesus came to forgive sin which means simply "to bear" or "to carry away" sin. For Him God was the Father of all men and women, even though they might ignore Him; and if all were sons, then all were also brothers, and sisters in Jesus Christ. Also common is the conception of sin as a sickness which God "heals" means (Forgives), "I will heal their backsliding, I will love them freely" Hos. 14:4; "I said, Lord, be merciful unto me: heal my soul; for I have sinned against thee." Psalm 41:4; 103:3.

But he was wounded for our transgressions, he was bruised for our iniquities: the chastisement of our peace was upon him; and with his stripes we are healed." Sickness and injury being so frequently conceived as God's judgment upon sin, his forgiveness could be expressed in terms of healing, usually accompanied by deliverance from the trouble.

The context of thought in this chapter has to do with the divine "repentance". The Hebrew word used for this repentance "naham" has as it basic meaning the conception of compassion, pity, and sorrow. Intercessory prayer furnished the condition in which God could show his compassion; thus he or she "repents", not in the sense that he or she changes his or her mind, but in the sense that the changed situation permits him or her to change his or her action from punishment to redemption. It should be notice that God's forgiverness is also granted when a human being or a people repents.

This is implicit in Matthew 25:41-45 regarding the Goats. The most common Hebrew expression for repent was the word "to turn" (shubh). Even in the midst of the gross sin of Jehoiakim's time 11 years reign, and like people today; if the people will "turn, every man from his evil way," God will forgive their sins and also read Isaiah 55:7.

It should be notice that the finally there is a forgiverness which God will grant at the end of the present era in the eschatological time when the conflicts of the present will be resolved. In this case the forgiveness is a free and unmerited act of God, independent of human repentance. Man or woman will be given a "new heart" so that his or her rebellion will cease, and God will forgive the sins of the past in Jer. 31:34; 33:8 and Isaiah 40:2; Ezek. 36:25-38.

These Scriptures portray the reconstitution of God's people as a sacred community in fellowship with himself. Forgiveness is both an intergral part and a consequence of this future redemption. It should be notice that Jesus spoken in verse 46 after death. The one area which this redemption faith of people had most difficulty in penetrating was that of the suffering and death of the individual man or woman.

The views of people regarding death were so strongly conditioned by those of Jesus Christ parables king, His disciples, and other, that the invasion and transformation of the realm by the new and unique theology of the Gospel was a slow process, completed in the come to an end. At death man or woman's unity of being is destroyed and he or she loses vitality. The soul does not continur to exist. It separate, or as in the case of the suffering servant, it is said to be poured out as an offering to death in Isaiah 53:12. The dead are like water spilt on the ground, which cannot be gathered up again in II Sam. 14:10.

This does not mean, however, that existence ceases. Man or woman continues to live, though in a very weak state, in the underworld of Hell, together with those who have passed into this realm before him. There he or she subsists in darkness, in a kind of sleep, in weakness, in forgetfulness. Existence in Hell thus was coneived as the opposite of life.

Earth is the land of light; Hell is filled with the primordial darkness in Gen. 1:2. Life means vitality and energy; death is weakness, inaction, a mere shadow of life. Since God is pre-eminently the giver of life and Lord of the living, it was something of a question to the people of this world; as to what relation he or she had with the dead. Is not death the separation from life and thus from the God of life? Consequently, the people questions whether God will show his wonders to the dead, whether his loving kindness and his righteousness will be known in the land of forgetfulness in Psalm 88:10-12; Isaiah 38:18. Before a person death the pastor or preach prays the more serious pray, therefore, to be delivered the soul from death's power. Many of the people lived in great danger of their lives or in grave illness; and any form of weakness which robbed them of the free exercise of their powers are to them a form of death, though as yet the gates of Hell had not closed finally upon them.

Their prayers were for God to save them and to bring them back from the "pit" or from the waves of the deep through which they have been forced to go in the journey to the underworld mean "Grave". It should be notice that in God's hands are the issues of life and death, for it is "The Lord killeth, and maketh alive: he bringeth down to the grave, and bringeth up." Deut. 32:39.

The faithful man or woman is certain, therefore, that God would redeem his or her life from Hell's power in Psalm 49:15; Hos. 13:14. Does this mean that death will be abolished? Such a statement as in Psalm 23:6 "I will dwell in the house of the Lord for ever" is somewhat ambiguous and unclear. There is no doubt, however, that during the lifespan period some believers began to answer the question in the affirmative.

In the parables that Jesus spoken about in Matt.25:33 "And he shall set the sheep on his right hand, but the goats on the left." In Jesus mind the right hand of a ruler has been considered a place of honor. Jesus own people will be placed there in recognition of what their actions have shown them to be.

In Jesus mind there shall be no more death, and tears shall be wiped away from all faces in Isaiah 25:8; I Cor. 15:26-54; Rev. 21:4. The diffaculty which the man or woman of faith had with death is that it separated him or her from life with God. Consequently, it is inevitable that sooner or later he or she would assert that the cause of this separation would be removed in Psalm 139:8, for God in life will guide him or her with his preacher and afterward received him with glory in Psalm 73:24.

A good illustration of the thought in the last passage was at hand in the cases of Enoch and Elijah, neither of whom suffered death but was taken directly to God's heavenly abode in Gen. 5:24; II Kings 2:11. This made it easier for some to believe that God would send Elijah back to earth again as the forerunner ofd the new age in Mal. 4:5; Mark 9:11-13.

If death is to be abolished by God in the Book of Revelation so that redeemed man or woman need never be separated from him or her; what about those who have died before they repent of their sin? The parables that Jesus gave Matt.25:33, and 25: 41-45, after the wonderful invitation extended to the "sheep" at His right, Jesus Christ turns to the "goats" on His left. It should be notice that this passage affirm Jesus resurrection, and their resurrection: Isaiah 26:19 and Daniel 12:2. In keeping with the unitary view of man or woman, this doctrine of the resurrection of the dead is the only one which would be congenial to the biblical point of view. Many People under the ultimate influence of Greek thought have felt it simpler to believe in the immortality of the soul, though from the standpoint of reason this separation of soul from body appears as difficult as the belief in the resurrection of the body, of the complete person.

To know God is to know Jesus Christ both in biblical history for the past, present, and future; the past and present reveals his intertion and will, the present will see his blessing, and future will see their fulfillment. We all should learn something from the parables of Jesus Christ in Matt. 25:31-46, that He will separation the "sheep" from the "Goats".

The concluded of this Chapter, the author looks forward to a time when God will intervene by raising up a man to restore peace and justice in the land. He will end strife and division, and in a united nation a life of security and happiness will again be possible for all. The roots of this hope lie far back in the past.

Indeed, we can trace them to the beginning of man, and to ancient Egypt. Author assigns to the period of political weakness ca. 2500 B.C., the yearning for social justice and for a strong ruler who will curb the rapacity of petty officialls and so ensure to every man or woman his or her rights.

We can distinguish two elements in the form taken here by this hope of an ideal ruler, one which we may well accept, another which we cannot. On the one hand, God works through a man who holds office and accepts public responsibility; the sphere of political action does not lie outside the Kingdon of God.

Rather can it provide the instruments and agents through which that kingdom is in some measure established among us. The God of the Holy Bible is the God who hears a cry and sends a man. But it is an error to suppose that God will use only the instruments accredited by the past.

Of course the writer anticipates that he will choose a scion of the legitimate dynasty and set up again the throne of David. But when the Good Shepherd comes at last, he does not base his claims on royal descent nor does he mount a throne. He is not concerned to restore the vanished glories of the brief but splendid empire over which David and Solomon ruled.

He comes rather to discharge the duties of the good shepherd, to heal the sick, blid up the injured, and lead home the wanderers. He accomplishes all this by means which no one recognized as royal till he made them peculiarly his own by his teaching, his cross, and his resurrection. For God fulfills himself as we need, not as we expect.

CHAPTER 6

The Angels of God

This Chapter give us only a few hints concerning the nature of Angels. The angels belonging to the sphere of heaven, they cannot be properly conceived in earthly terms. They are almost always described in relation to God, as His angels. Even the two angelic names Michael and Gabriel emphasize this relationship.

In Hebrews, they are described as (Ministering Spirits), in a conflation of the two parts of Psalms. Elsewhere, in the book of Job and the book of Psalms, they are called the (Heavenly Ones), or (Saints) God's service, (Sons of God) and (God). Since Christians can also be called the Sons of God, we need not infer from the latter phrases, as did some of the apologists; that they are lesser deities.

The term which the Bible uses to describe angels gives us the clue to the function by which they are primarily to be known and understood. They are the ambassadors of God. They belong to his heavenly court and service. Their mission in heaven is to praise Him, and to do His will; and in this mission they behold his face.

But since heaven comes down to earth, they also have a mission on the earth; accompanying God in his work of creation. In fulfilment of this mission their task is to declare the word of God, and to do his work. The function of angels is best seen from their part in the saving mission of Jesus Christ.

It is natural that they should be present bothe when he came to each and at his resurrection and ascension. They are also to accompany him at his return in glory. They don't do the real work of reconciliation. But they declare and accompany, and they summon man to participate in their work of praise. It is interesting that between the nativity and the resurrection there seem to be only two angelic appearances in the ministry of Jesus, at the beginning of his way to the cross in the temptation and at its culmination in Gethsemane. This is perhaps due to the fact that Jesus Christ must tread this way alone; and that in his huiliation he is made a little lower than the angels.

Angels a heavenly messenger, one of the types of apiritual attendants of God; believed to convey the authority of the sender as if he himself were present. In some passages it is difficult to determine whether it is God's angel that appears to man. Belief in angels was prevalent in Biblical times and was accepted by Jesus in his teaching.

They were generally thought of as (Blameless) and (Sons of God). The seven angels that stand in the presence of God; in definite article suggests that we should regard these as the seven archangels and angels. They are Gabriel, Michael, Raphael, Jeremiel, Raguel, Remiel, Saraqael, and Uriel, they are mentioned in Enoch books of Apocrypha. Only Gabriel and Michael are named in the Bible.

1. Gabriel is a archangels angels, a angels of man of God, or God has shown himself mighty. One of the seven archangels in the Hebrew celestial (hierarchy) akin to the Babylonian and Persian counter parts. Gabriel's function was that of a revealing messenger from God. To Daniel he explained a vision and a decree in Daniel 8:15; 9:21. To Zacharias and Elisabeth, Gabriel announced the coming of a son and declared his name in Luke 1:5,17. To Mary he heralded the birth of a son and announced his name in Luke 1:26, 38, and Luke 1:19.

2. Michael is a archangels angels, who is like God, the name of severed men mentioned in I Chronicles, none of whom was outstanding; and of a son of king Jehoshahat of Israel in II Chronicles. An angels of the Persion period, mentioned in Daniel 10:13, 21; 12:1, as guarding Israelites against the influences of Persia and Greece.

    In Jude, where he is an archangel contending with the devil to secure the body of Moses in Deut. 34:6; Rev. 12:7, where he at war with the dragon of evil Satan. All will agree that the beginning with the verse 7-12, provides the explanation as to why the dragon has turned on the woman and cause her to flee into the desert for protection.

His action is in two parts: (1) the battle in heaven between Michael and his angels and the dragon and his angels, which results in the ejection of Satan from heaven to the earth. (2) the heavenly hymn of victory. As elsewhere in Revelation, the material can be interpreted only in the light of the hymns.

This principle is especially important in verse 7-9, where the victory takes place in heaven as the result of Michael's defeat of the dragon. Were this the only thing told us about the (war in heaven), it might be concluded that the dragon's defeat was unrelated to Jesus Christ. But the interpretative hymn says that it was in fact the blood of Christ that dealt the actual death blow to the dragon and enabled the saints to triumph.

Does this not suggest that the redeeming work of Christ is here depicted by the cosmic battle of Michael, and the dragon as it is elsewhere seen as a loosing from sin, as a washing of our garment, and as a purchasing to God. Early Judaism (Jewish) belief held the view that Michael would cast Satan from heaven as the first of the last time struggles to establish the Kingdom of God on earth.

3. Raphael is a archangels angels, and is one of the principal characters in the book of Tobit(in the Apocrypha), and he say, "I am Raphael, one of the seven Holy Angels, which go in before the glory of the HOLY ONE."

4. Jeremiel is a archangels angels are mentioned in Enoch books of Apocrypha. Jeremiel is a warrior who battle against Satan, and his angels in heaven, and on the earth.

5. Raguel is a archangels angels are mentioned in Enoch books of Apocrypha. Raguel is a warrior who battle against Satan and his angels in heaven, and on the earth.

6. Remiel is a archangels angels are mentioned in Enoch books of Apocrypha. Remiel is a warrior who battle against Satan and his angels in heaven, and on the earth.

7.   Saraqael is a archangels angels are mentioned in Enoch books of Apocrypha. Saraqael is a warrior who battle against Satan and his angels in heaven, and on the earth.

8.   Uriel is a archangels angels, the light of God, one of the archangels angels. A prominent Kokathite Levite who helped bring the ark from the home of obededom to Jerusalem in I Chron. 6:24; 15:5,11.

The seven angels that stand in the presence of God; in definite article suggests that we should regard these as the eight archangels. The eight angels of mankind protection. The angels begin to watch over mankind when He God said to Abraham, "And I will make of thee a great nation, and I will bless thee, and make thy name great; and thou shalt be a blessing." Gen. 12:2.

This suggests that God from the beginning forms the concluding paragraph of the book of the covenant, but originally was directed from Sinai to the Chidren of Abraham as they set out toward the Promised Land. God remains in Sinai but his word to Abraham is, "I send an Angel before thee."

The implication of the whole passage is that if people had obeyed the law of God, and walked in his ways, its people would have been the happiest people on earth. God had looked after everything for them. It is a sober truth for us all. God has anticipated and looked after everything for us.

It depends entirely upon us whether we walk in the way of peace or stray into the byways of distress. God said, "I will be an enemy unto thine enemies, and an adversary unto thine adversaries, God shall bless thy bread, and thy water, By little and little, I will drive, thine enemies out from before thee, until thou, inherit the land." Well, what more could you ask?

God will take care of you. But there are conditions you must cooperate with God: Please note, "you must obey the voice of God angels", and you must not worship the gods of the enemy, you shall not let the gods of the hearhen ensnare you, nor make any covenant with them, but be wholly a sincere servant of God." This is testimony of all people in all ages group.

Sometime God would let us experience danger, it may cause harm or injury. In the case of Balaam in Number 22.20, "And God came unto Balaam at night, and said unto him, If the men come to call thee, rise up, and go with them; but yet the word which I shall say unto thee, that shalt thou do." It is clear that Balaam listen to Balak that morning his saddled his ass, and went with the princes of Moab.

It would seem that there is some warrant for dealing with Bal-aam quite apart from the main strands of the Balaam behavior. It obviously presents a less favorable attitude toward Balaam by some scholar. On no other grounds can we say why God should be angry with Balaam when God warned Balaam before hand.

Remember verse 20, "And God came unto Balaam at night, and said unto him." God can to warned him, Balaam disregard God's word. To deal with the incident recorded in this case as a story, or a dream, or a vision, should not cancel the implication for us of the angel that blocks the way. In one form or another do we not have spiritual experiences similar to that of Balaam?

Like we are often blind to these hindering angels, and like him we becaome indignant when others who are sensitive to their presence tell us they are there. God send his angel to Balaam, "Then the Lord opened the eyes of Balaam, and he saw the angel of the Lord standing in the way, with his drawn sword in his hand." Surely we need to have our eyes opened to these angels who block the way, who are sent to hinder us and thus to help us.

Does not Christ himself open our eyes to them? This case seems appropriate for Advent, when our thoughts naturally turn to angels, the messengers of his coming Jesus Christ. If we listen to the angels of God, we will see the righteous thing. We will knew that righteousness, being right with God and right with man and woman, makes it quite all right with a man or woman when he or she meets death. But as Christians we also know that a righteous life with Jesus Christ carries within itself the assurance of life after death.

If we listen to the angels of God. We will covet such an end for ourselves we must begin with Jesus Christ now and continue with him till journey's end which leads at hast to the Father's God house. To be sure, the beneficiaries of his protection are his own people. Record to King David,

> "The chariots of God are twenty thousand, even thousands of angels: the Lord is among them, as in Sinai, in holy place."

Psalm 68:17.

King David says, "Praise ye the Lord. Praise ye the Lord from the heavens: praise him in the heights." In heven the issues are clear; the motives are not mingled. A living face is seen, not an image in a dark glass. Therefore angelic praise is purer, the shouts louder, the phrases triumphant, and the joy exalted.

It is good for men, women, and children to remember that there is a mighty unseen company not merely submissive to his will, but rejoicing in it as the highest happiness and the perfect freedom. One generation of the whole earth in revolt provides not enough voices to drown out the heavenly choir. So the angels of the psalmist the Christian now adds the mighty company of the redeemed, the great clouds of wtnesses, saints, apostles, prophets, and martyrs.

Over all the discordant medley of the earth, that added, harmonious praise in heaven, "Glory to God in the highest, and on earth peace, good will toward men." Even the sun and moon and shining stars join with the angels. Behind this appeal to the powers of nature lies the primitive feeling that once they were living beings who could offer conscious praise.

To modern man, and woman, scientifically analytical, they have no voices, no breath, no tongues, no lips; but yet they declare the glory of God. The Angels of God is our protection. Angels Gabriel can to give good new to Zacharias about him and his wife Elisabeth shall bear him a son, and his name is John.

Zacharias did not believe the word from Gabriel. The angel said,

> "I am Gabriel, that stand in the presence of God; and am
> sent to speak unto thee, and to shew thee these glad tidings."
> Luke 1:19-20. Verse 20, "And, behold thou shalt be dumb,
> and not able to speak, until the day that these things shall
> be performed, because thou believest not my words, which
> shall be fulfilled in their season."

The Angels of God is an agent of God, his message to the people, and protection. Angel appears in Greek literature as early as Homer. In primitive Greek thought the term referred both to a personal agent and an impersonal force. Furthermore it was used primarily of a personal agent in a religious or secular role for the Isaelite. Angels play only a restricted role in the Israelite tradition prior to the time of the Babylonian exile. The Isaelite experience in exile, however, affected the concept in two respects. It stimulated the development of strict monotheism a perspective which led to the concept of angels as mediators, and it provided access to Iranian and Babylonian terminology and cosmology to express the concept of angels.

Although the development of the doctrine of angels in Jewish thought was not uniform, a full-orbed angelology is evident in specific areas of Jewish literature, particularly in no biblical material. Angels play an important role in Apocalpytic thought as revealers of esteric information. Scattered references to angels appear in Hebrew language but their role is carefully circumscribed. Most Jewish interpreters understand references to angels as poetic symbolism or as obsolete remains of an earlier cosmology.

Christians adopted Judaism beliefs about angels, but the doctrine of The Holy Spirit set definite limits to the development of Christian angelology. Angels are frequently mentioned in the New Testament in Luke 1-2; I Thess. 4:16; Rev. 16:1-17, but tendencies toward angel worship were subjected to a sharp citique in Col. 2:8-10.

Some scholar said that Pseudo-Dionysius(six century A.D.) development a heavenly hierarchy from seraphim at the top to archangels and angels at the bottom. Most popular ideas about angels stem from him, not the Bible. In European religious art also reflects his influence, though classical putti were the inspiration for "cherubs." Various attempts have been made to restate Jewish, and Christian angelology.

Psychoanalysis points to structures of personality that are analogous to the tripartite structure of the universe assumed by angelology. In some citcles belief in angels is supported by appeal to the literal meaning of the scripture or to earlier teachings of the church. However, since the Copernican revolution they are commonly understood as elements of an obsolete cosmology.

We all of God's people, and we need to be protection by the Angels of God from the "Evil One Satan."

PRAYERS TO HUMANITY

O God you are great from eternity, you have knowledge of what is hidden, you created everything by the power of your word; you guide and control all things by the gentle movement of your will, always bring to effect much more than we ask or imagine, in accordance with power which works within us; you acquired your holy church, establishing in it Apostles, Prophets, Pastor, Priests and Teachers through whom you might increase that knowledge of the truth which your only begotten Son gave to Humanity.

O Lord, make your face to shine now as well upon this servant of yours, making his election Holy through the anointing of the Holy Spirit, so that we may be a perfect ministry, one who imitates the true high God who gave His life for our sakes.

Strengthen him with the spirit of Holiness in this ministry which He is entering; grant to him, O God the Father of Truth, all holy and glorious, That he may shepherd your people with an upright heart, preaching the unerring word of truth, may we be a source of light to those who sit in darkness, a guide for the uncertain, a teacher for the young and the children, and all mankind to love each other; to you and to me and to the Holy Spirit let us offer up praise, honour, thanksgiving and worship, now and for eternal ages. Amen.

CONCLUSION

We hope we have been able to draw certain lines of connection between some very ancient themes defining the human condition with reference to GOOD and EVIL. Some immediate developments with special referenced to the orientations, functions, and obligations of the contempt the universadistic thrust of modern values.

Our primary these are, first, that the problem of the meaning of Good and Evil has been continued coming more and more explicitly to the fore in the recent years of development of our culture, and that a major focus of this Evil has been in the World.

Second, we feel that old as these developments are, they are not understandable except in reference to the Jewish and the Christian faith of our culture, especially as expressed as Good and Evil. The theme of gift exchange between God and man has been central to our analysis.

In particular, we have emphasized the Good of the conception that human life is a gift from God. So it is with God's moral law; it reveals what sin is, it declares all men or women to be guilty before God; but it cannot remove guilt or sin. Only the grace of Lord Jesus Christ can do that.

That why Jesus Christ forgive, us stop blaming or feeling anger toward a persons. The restoration of fellowship where sin has caused on estrangement, has both a human and divine aspect. The idea of forgiveness appears early, as in the quest of the aged Jacob. Forgiveness is available to him or her whose trespass was unintentional.

Forgiveness is the only way to salvation, the only channel through which the sinned who has offended the righteous nature of God can return to fellowship. God must take the initiative, although man or woman, through his or her penitence, prepares himself or herself for the divine approach. Occasionally, however, instances occur in Scripture where individuals other than the sinner intercede with God for forgiveness, as in Solomon's prayer at the dedication of the temple. And the matchless intercession of Christ's on his cross for those who had put him there. The letter incident implies that the repentance of sinner is not essential to the extension of forgiveness.

The idea is generally expounded, that Jesus Christ interceded on behalf of sinner, God will hear that plea out of consideration for him or her who had been injured. This is certainly one of the most sublime ideas found anywhere in sacred literature. Forgiveness is the high peak in the ethics of Jesus Christ.

It is best expressed in his parable of the unmerciful debtor. Jesus made it clear that the sinner's forgiveness by God was dependent upon his or her own willingness to forgive whose who had wronged him. The question as to whether God or Jesus, had power to forgive sins aroused hearted controversy in Jesus day.

The answer is stated in Jesus Christ own words. Mark and John, suggests that Jesus delegated to his disciples to forgive sins. The issue of forgiveness is not adjudication of the church, still less absolute granting of forgiveness by the church. Only God or Jesus Christ can forgive sins in so absolute aways.

Peter came to Jesus and asked, Lord, How many times shall I forgive my borther when he sins against me? Jesus response 70x-70=77, but Jesus is not saying that seventy seven times is upper limit, that the forgiveness is fifty unqualified it vitiates the discipline and procedural steps just taught.

No book of Christianity except the Bible teaches that God completely forgiven sin. But, we reads, "I will heal their backslidings, I will love them freely." For Jesus sake, God hath forgiven you of all your sins. There is only one sin for which God will not promise forgiveness; "Blasphemy" against the "Holy Ghost."

The theme suggests this to be the sin of attributing to unclean spirit's the work of the Holy Spirit. This sin is also considered by some to be the unforgiving spirit. It might be the sin unto death; there are to be no limitations whatever to forgiveness of oneself. It is to be seven times in a day, and until seventy times seven. Both of which signify limitlessness, it is to be an attitude of mind even before the offending party asks for pardon as in implied by Jesus Christ.

"We should forgive from the heart." For we to receive forgiveness, repentance is necessary." For Jesus to extend forgiveness, the shedding of blood on the cross. Repentance in the Old Testament means turning to God. In turning to God, however, the penitent also turns away from something from that which he or she has come to realize is displeasing to God.

The act is accompanied by sorrow for that which makes the repentance necessary. If there is not this sorrow for the evil deed or for the evil condition, then there is no true repentance.

How earnestly the great prophets called on the people to turn away from evil to God may be seen. "Turn ye, turn ye from your evil ways, for why will ye die, O house of Israel? In fact, the Hebrew words for turn is only occasionally translated repent in the English Versions; turn is the common translation and it is the themes that usually shows that the turning involves repentance.

In the New Testament, we are taught that God will change his attitude toward men and women, when certain conditions are met. This indeed, is the consistent message of the New Testament. But in respect to the themes Good and Evil, his purpose, God does not change.

James expressed this truth exactly when he writes that God is one with whom can be no variableness, neither shadow that is cast by turning. The New Testament, however, has much to say about human repentance. When it differs chiefly from the Old Testament is in the understanding of sin.

The act of turning depends on the revelation which God has made of himself in Jesus Christ. What men or woman take to be sin depends on their belief concerning God and his or her purpose there are necessarily degrees of repentance because there are degrees of understanding of God. There are certain gross, and palpable sins which are widely recognized as such; it is no matter for surprise that David should repent for adultery and murder.

There were only sins, they were crimes as well; but people or Christians repentance is by no means limited to crime or to what is often called sin of the flesh. But in the New Testament there is special emphasis on the state of the inner life. Men and women are called on to repent not merely for the evil things they do, but for their evil thoughts and purposes, and for that in themselves which leads them to evil.

The standard of goodness in the New Testament is nothing less than Christ himself as the revelation of God's character and will and this yields a corresponding standard for sin. Jesus Christ here, contrast the state of the heart with the outer deed. One may desire to do evil, but for prudential reasons may abstain, Jesus Christ taught thast such a man or woman had already done the evil in his or her heart.

Jesus say, Christian should pray daily for forgiveness. The mood of repentance is a normal Christian mood. The more the believe sees himself or herself in the imperfection. Remember the subject of the preaching of John the Baptist, preaching a baptism of repentance for the remission of sin and forgiveness of sin.

Jesus Christ continues John's subject but, adds, significantly, "The time is fulfilled" his coming is the coming of the Kingdom in person and decisive; all life relationship must be clean. The preaching of repentance and remission of sins must be joined to the proclamation of the cross and the resurrection. All Christian are true to this commission, but unfaithful or evil person or Christian must repent. But in any serious situation or when Good and Evil; there is no competent. This book can help you to be a better person, when you read it; it will also enable you to understand Good and Evil.

As you read through this book, you will get better idea of what Good is, what Evil things, that sin cause men and women to have diseases. Read with understanding and prayer for guidance you through a better life. I overcome fear because fear is evil. Have no fear! Fear is evil and perfect love casts out fear. There is no room for fear in the heart in which God dwell. Fear destroys Hope.

It cannot exist where "Love" is, or where "Faith" is. Fear is the curse of the world. Man or woman is afraid of poverty, afaid of loneliness, afraid of unemployment, afraid of sickness. Many are men or women fears. Nation is afraid of nation. Fear everywhere. Fight fear as you would a plague.

Turn it out of your lives, your home, your church, and your community. Fight it singly, fight it together. Never insoire fear. It is an evil ally. Fear of punishment, fear of blame. No work that employs this enemy of mine is work for God. Banish it. There must be another and better way.

Ask God, and He will show it to you. When the Bible says, "God has purer eyes than to behold evil", it means to impute evil to His people. How always sees the good in people, but remember that god: Beheld the city and wept over it".

GLOSSARY

Abomination is offensive to God and His plan for man's righteous way of life. pp. 17

Abomination of Desolation in both words referred to several time is Daniel and Revelation as an apocalyptic figure, idol or expression of an idea set up in the sanctuary which baleful effect. pp. 17

Alcoholism is called strong drink, caused intoxicating liquor. pp. 21

Anger is generally means wrath and indignation are integral to the biblical proclamation of the living God's His opposition to sin. pp. 61

Antichrist is an antagonist of christ who denies that Jesus in the Christ. pp. 16

Beast is used symbolically in Deniel and Revelation for empires and powers hostile to God and His people. pp. 16

Blindness was often attributed to sin. pp. 23

Cancer is a malignant tumor or growth of various structural characteristics which may develop in any tissue or organ. pp. 28

Covetousness means primarily inordinate desire. pp. 56

Cutaneous disease it's affecting the skin. pp. 28

Demon among the Greeks a demon was originally, as in Homer, a god or deity, and the word is used once in this sense in the New Testament.

The angels "Demons" that are bound are evidently guilty or more heinous wickedness and are incarcerated in Jartarus. pp. 13

Devil is the personification of wickedness, incarnate evil. pp. 15

Dragon a mythical monster depicted in the literature of the ancient Middle East. pp. 16

Dropsy is an abnormal accumulation of serious fluid in the tissues of the body. pp. 29

Dumbness is lacking the power of speech; mute or unwilling to talk. pp. 30

Dysentery is any of various intestinal inflammation characterized by abdominal pain and intense diarrhea with bloody. pp. 30

El is the divine being, the highest God, Possessor or Creator of heaven and earth. pp. 4

Endocrine is disturbances is any gland producing one or more internal secretion that are introduced directly into the bloodstream and carried to other parts of the body whose functions they regulate or control. pp. 30

Envy is always means bad, jealously, and zeal are frequently good: similarly to eye and the evil eye. pp. 59

Epilepsy is a chronic disease of the nervous system. pp. 30

Evil one is the antithesis of good, and the possibility of its eradication from the soul of man, were prominent in the thought of the minds which produced the Bible. pp. 15

Eye diseases is Xanthelasma are somewhat elevated, yellow deposits in the skin of the lids. pp. 31

Fever is the rise of body temperature above the normal 98.6 F. pp. 31

Glutton is a person who greedily eats too much; a person with a great capacity for something. pp. 60

Goats is the unrighteousness people in the parables of Jesus Christ in Matthew 25:33. pp. 63

God as Creator in the Bible open with the account of God's creating the universe. pp. 6

Gonorrhea is an acute, contagious venereal disease most commonly contracted through sexual intercourse, mostly promiscuous. pp. 31

Gout is said to be a disease of the well-to-do, and of the over fed, also of those who indulge in alcoholic liquors, and especially in the fermented beer or wines. pp. 32

I am that I am: that is to say, God is One's who exists and who can never cease to exist. pp. 5

Jehovah is the redemptive name of God. pp. 4

Jesus Christ: The eternal Father gives from within Himself His eternal Son to redeem men and women from bondage, set free, from a power greater than themselves, and it is this that God sets himself to accomplish in Jesus Christ. pp. 7

Lucifer is a name given the planet Venus when it is the morning star. Lucifer is a name given by God the "shining one" and Jesus saying, I beheld Satan as lightning fall from heaven." Lucifer came to be regarded as the name of Satan before his fall. pp. 15

Lameness is disqualified a man from becoming a priest of Yahweh. pp. 32

Leprosy is an infectious disease, but it does not seem to be catching like other contagious disease. pp. 32

Lust is a desire to gratify the senses; bodily appetite sexual desire as seeking unrestrained gratification. pp. 57

Malaria is a parasitic disease cause by the plasmodium of which there are several varieties. pp. 33

Mental disorders is report that a virus or germ of such a common infection as rheumatism may invade the arteries of the brain and give rise to the mental illness psychiatrists cell by the cabalistic name schizophrenia. pp. 33

Paralysis is loss of sensation and motion is a part of the body is termed paralysis. pp. 34

Pestilence a Bubonic Plaque is a fatal infection characterized by the appearance of enlarged, painful lymphatic gland (buboes) attaining the size of a walnut. pp. 34

Plagues: The plagues, the Scripture to indicate (a) an affliction or a calamity viewed as a visitation from God. pp. 35

The Ten's Plagues of Egypt. pp. 35

Pride may be defined as inordinate and unreasonably, self-esteem, attended with insolence and rude Treatment of other. pp. 35

Redemption, the root meaning of the word, redeem "TO SET FREE" or "TO CAUSE TO BE SET FREE". pp. 6

Satan is an high angelic creature who, before the creation of the human race, rebelled against the Creator and became the chief antagonist of God and man. pp. 15

Serpent is an snake, the serpent of the Garden of Eden; a symbol of evil, and Satan. 17

Sheep is the righteousness people in the parables of Jesus Christ in Matthew 25:33. pp. 63

Sloth is the general term refer to extremely dull, unresponsive, or inactive states due to laziness, sluggish health, or mental depression. pp. 62

Sunstroke heart prostration is a condition affecting overworked and weak individual when over-hearted. pp. 40

Trinity is the union of three divine Persons in the Godhead. pp. 6

Thrombocytopenia (ITP): This cause the blood cells known as platelets play a vital part in the mechanisms of the body that stop bleeding. pp. 45

Worms an larvae of insects which eat organic matter, like bread, or wool, or the human body, and vegetable. pp. 42

Yhwh (Yahweh). The Hebrew name for God. pp. 4

INDEX TO SCRIPTURE REFERENCE

(All Biblical Source are from the King James Version)

Nehemiah 9:6
Job 26:14
Job 1:1-2-7
Psalms 91:10
Psalms 73:6
Proverbs 23:32
Proverbs 26:25
Proverbs 23:30-31-32
Proverbs 23:29
Proverbs 12:24-27
Proverbs 13:19
Proverbs 23:21
Proverbs 6:17
Ecclesiastes 10:18
Ecclesiastes 14:8-10
Isaiah 45:7
Isaiah 14:12
Isaiah 14:29
Isaiah 40:18
Isaiah 1:6
Jeremiah 21:6
Jeremiah 49:16
Ezekiel 6:11
Ezekiel 6:12
Daniel 9:27
Daniel 12:11
Daniel 10:13
Daniel 18:13

The New Testament

Daniel 11:31
Daniel 5:20
Jonah 4:7
Micah 6:10
Zechariah 3:1-2
Matthew 12:24
Matthew 7:10
Matthew 25:41
Matthew 9:32-33
Matthew 17:15
Matthew 4:24
Matthew 12:10
Matthew 3:7
Matthew 26:28
Matthew 2:18
Matthew 9:20
Matthew 5:28
Matthew 20:15
Matthew 11:19
Matthew 25:26
Matthew 25:31-46
Mark 13:14
Mark 2:3-5
Mark 7:22
Mark 8:26
Mark 1:40-41